MW01059139

"Scripture is for sound doctrine, sound doctrine is for real life, and real life is for real church growth. So says Jamieson, and he hits the nail on the head brilliantly every time."

J. I. Packer, Board of Governors, Professor of Theology, Regent College

"'Pay heed to your doctrine.' That imperative for faithful Christianity sounds to many Christians altogether abstract and remote from the life of the church. Bobby Jamieson believes otherwise, and *Sound Doctrine* is a masterful argument for doctrine that is not only deeply rooted in the church, but also produces a church that demonstrates both the grace and glory of God."

R. Albert Mohler Jr., President, The Southern Baptist Theological Seminary

"A true Christian experience involves more than sound doctrine, but it is nothing without it. Bobby helps us see how sound doctrine not only shapes but also empowers all ministries in the local church, from effective outreach to authentic small groups. This book could serve as a starting point for thinking through a philosophy of ministry."

J. D. Greear, Lead Pastor, The Summit Church, Durham, North Carolina; author, *Stop Asking Jesus into Your Heart: How to Know for Sure You Are Saved*

"Truth is for life. Teaching is for living. Sound doctrine is for love, unity, worship, witness, and joy. That is what this book is all about. Christians need to understand how sound biblical teaching—doctrine that is based on and drawn from the Holy Scriptures—informs every aspect of Christian life and experience. Bobby Jamieson makes that case in *Sound Doctrine*. The argument is brief, biblical, interesting, and compelling. The book won't take you long to read, but its contents will pay dividends to Christians and churches for a long time to come."

J. Ligon Duncan, Chancellor, CEO, and John E. Richards Professor of Systematic and Historical Theology, Reformed Theological Seminary

"Do you think doctrine is at least impractical—at worst, loveless? Give this author a few minutes to help you reconsider this. Well-written, precise, provocative, and practical—Jamieson has produced a jewel."

Mark Dever, Senior Pastor, Capitol Hill Baptist Church, Washington, DC

"I sit next to Bobby Jamieson in a seminary class, so I can tell you that he is a very smart guy, a genuine nerd, theologically discerning, and—surprisingly—an avid surfer. Prior to my conversion, I sat next to smart guys like Bobby in order to cheat, but now I do it to learn—and there's a lot to learn from Bobby! If you don't understand why sound doctrine is important, or realize the difference it can make, then Bobby has something to teach you. In this book you'll learn that sound doctrine is as delightful as it is practical—for everyday life and for the church. Come sit next to Bobby with me."

C. J. Mahaney, Senior Pastor, Sovereign Grace Church of Louisville

"Doctrine that is biblically faithful and practically relevant is essential to the health and life of the church. Without it, churches will become anemic and eventually die. *Sound Doctrine* is a short primer on the key doctrines of holiness, love, unity, worship, and witness. In a careful and well-written treatise, Bobby Jamieson walks us through these crucial doctrines, revealing their importance to our mind and heart—to our individual lives and the community of faith."

Daniel L. Akin, President, Southeastern Baptist Theological Seminary

"If ever you've been tempted to think that doctrine is boring, divisive, or just plain pointless, this is a book for you. Bobby Jamieson shows that sound doctrine is beautiful, life imparting, and deeply desirable. I hope this message goes far and wide."

Michael Reeves, President and Professor of Theology, Union School of Theology, Oxford, UK; author, *Delighting in the Trinity* and *The Unquenchable Flame*

Chapter 1 Sound Doctrine is for Life. Life in the church

pg 22: Scripture teaches us that Christianity is much more like a team sport. It is true that each of us must grow individually

§ 25 The gospel teaches us to put others before ourselves, and to use the strengths God has given us to edify our fellow church members - both of which are impossible to do alone.

§ 25 What a church does together defines the life of a church.

Chapter 2 S.D. is for reading + teaching the Bible!

§ 36 God's character matters for how we live.

§ SD has a lot to do w/ Systematic Theology as well as biblical theology... pg 39 helps us put together bible as a whole, which is a crucial step to applying for our lives.

p. 44 SD is for reading + teaching the bible in the church and for doing theology in the community.

Chapter 3 C.J. Mahaney guest at Grace Community Church 3500 Worship center pg 51 God used sound doctrine to produce

Chapter 4! pg 67 John wants these Christians united in a love that flows from the truth. Therefore they must not allow false teaching to enter their assembly and hack away at the roots of their love.

§ 69 Sound doctrine provides pattern for our love... Christ

Chapter 5 pg 76 Unity in the church is foundational, flows from the doctrine of justification by faith alone. pg 78 - Ephesians 4 unity in One God

pg 81 unity around sound doctrine, not politics, etc.

Chapter 6 Worship is about God. Not us. pg 85

Chapter 7. pg 95 The practice is for performance, for witness.
Sound doctrine frames the gospel, helping pg 100. Send doctrine us to explain it + make sense of it. Sound doctrine is for witness.

SOUND DOCTRINE

Building Healthy Churches series

Series Editors: Mark Dever and Jonathan Leeman

Biblical Theology: How the Church Faithfully Teaches the Gospel,
   Nick Roark and Robert Cline

Church Elders: How to Shepherd God's People Like Jesus,
   Jeramie Rinne

Church Discipline: How the Church Protects the Name of Jesus,
   Jonathan Leeman

*Church Membership: How the World Knows Who Represents
   Jesus*, Jonathan Leeman

Conversion: How God Creates a People, Michael Lawrence

Discipling: How to Help Others Follow Jesus, Mark Dever

Evangelism: How the Whole Church Speaks of Jesus,
   J. Mack Stiles

Expositional Preaching: How We Speak God's Word Today,
   David Helm

The Gospel: How the Church Portrays the Beauty of Christ,
   Ray Ortlund

Missions: How the Local Church Goes Global, Andy Johnson

Prayer: How Praying Together Shapes the Church,
   John Onwuchekwa

*Sound Doctrine: How a Church Grows in the Love and Holiness
   of God*, Bobby Jamieson

BUILDING HEALTHY CHURCHES

SOUND DOCTRINE

HOW A
CHURCH GROWS
IN THE LOVE
AND HOLINESS
OF GOD

BOBBY JAMIESON

WHEATON, ILLINOIS

Sound Doctrine: How a Church Grows in the Love and Holiness of God

Copyright © 2013 by Robert B. Jamieson III

Published by Crossway
    1300 Crescent Street
    Wheaton, Illinois 60187

Cover design: Dual Identity inc.

Cover image: Wayne Brezinka for brezinkadesign.com

First printing 2013

Printed in the United States of America

Hardcover ISBN: 978-1-4335-3589-5
PDF ISBN: 978-1-4335-3590-1
Mobipocket ISBN: 978-1-4335-3591-8
epub ISBN: 978-1-4335-3592-5

Library of Congress Cataloging-in-Publication Data

Jamieson, Bobby, 1986–
Sound doctrine : how a church grows in the love and holiness of God / Bobby Jamieson.
        p. cm. — (9marks)
Includes bibliographical references and index
    ISBN 978-1-4335-3589-5 (hc)
1. Church growth. 2. Theology, Doctrinal. I. Title.
BV652.25.J36   2013
250—dc23   2012037604

Crossway is a publishing ministry of Good News Publishers.

LB		29	28	27	26	25	24	23	22	21	20	19
14	13	12	11	10	9	8	7	6	5	4	3	2

For Kristin,
with all my love.

CONTENTS

For what use is it to know the truth in words,
only to defile the body and perform evil deeds?
Or what profit indeed can come from holiness of body,
if truth is not in the soul? For these rejoice together
and join forces to lead man to the presence of God.

IRENAEUS OF LYONS,
ON THE APOSTOLIC PREACHING[1]

[1] Irenaeus of Lyons, *On the Apostolic Preaching* (Crestwood, NY: St. Vladimir's Seminary Press, 1997), 40.

SERIES PREFACE

The 9Marks series of books is premised on two basic ideas. First, the local church is far more important to the Christian life than many Christians today perhaps realize.

Second, local churches grow in life and vitality as they organize their lives around God's Word. God speaks. Churches should listen and follow. It's that simple. When a church listens and follows, it begins to look like the One it is following. It reflects his love and holiness. It displays his glory. A church will look like him as it listens to him.

So our basic message to churches is, don't look to the best business practices or the latest styles; look to God. Start by listening to God's Word again.

Out of this overall project comes the 9Marks series of books. Some target pastors. Some target church members. Hopefully all will combine careful biblical examination, theological reflection, cultural consideration, corporate application, and even a bit of individual exhortation. The best Christian books are always both theological and practical.

It's our prayer that God will use this volume and the others to help prepare his bride, the church, with radiance and splendor for the day of his coming.

INTRODUCTION

What do you think about doctrine? Does it only cause fights and divisions between Christians? Does it distract us from the real work of evangelism? Is it important for pastors but not really anybody else?

Maybe you have a more positive attitude toward doctrine. Maybe you love learning about God, but sometimes it seems that your head is growing much faster than your heart.

Whatever your stance toward doctrine, the goal of this book is to convince you that sound doctrine is essential for living godly lives and building healthy churches. Why? Because sound doctrine is for life—the life of the church.

There are two main ideas that run through this book. The first is that sound doctrine is for life. That is, it's practical. It's not a set of abstract facts, but a road map that shows us who we are, where we are, and where we're going. Therefore, sound doctrine is essential for living lives and building churches that bring glory to God.

The second main idea of this book is that sound doctrine is for the life *of the church.* That is, sound doctrine produces lives that are shaped like a healthy local church. The fruits which sound doctrine nourishes are not merely individual, but corporate. Therefore, sound doctrine is essential for every aspect of the corporate lives of our churches.

This means that as we as individual Christians study sound doctrine, we should constantly apply what we learn in our local churches. And it means that pastors should faithfully nourish their flocks with sound doctrine, and should shape every aspect of their churches around sound doctrine. Doctrine isn't just for a statement of faith that's hidden away on a back page of a church website; it's for sermons, small groups, personal conversations, prayers, songs, and more. Sound doctrine should course through our churches' veins and nourish every aspect of our lives together.

This book has its roots in a Bible study I wrote called *The Whole Truth about God: Biblical Theology*.[1] The contents have grown and evolved, but if you want to explore some of this material in a Sunday school or small-group context, you can check out that study.

We'll begin in chapter 1 by establishing that sound doctrine is for life—the life of the church. Chapter 2 focuses on how sound doctrine shapes how we read and teach the Bible, both as individuals and in the church. The rest of the book examines five fruits in the life of the church that sound doctrine feeds and nourishes: holiness, love, unity, worship, and witness.

Are you ready? Good. Me too.

---

[1] *The Whole Truth about God: Biblical Theology* (Wheaton, IL: Crossway, 2012). This Bible study is part of a ten-volume set called the 9Marks Healthy Church Study Guides, all published by Crossway.

1

SOUND DOCTRINE IS FOR LIFE—THE LIFE OF THE CHURCH

I've always had a thing for maps. When I was a little kid and my family went on a road trip, I'd monitor our progress from the back seat, eagerly poring over the easel-sized *Rand McNally Road Atlas* that sprawled over my lap. Call me a nerd if you like, but it sure beat asking, "Are we there yet?" every five minutes.

Of course, the lines-on-paper variety aren't the only useful kind of maps. We all make mental maps that help us do the things we need to do—like pick up groceries, run to Target, and drop off library books, all before the little one's nap time—or do the things we love.

I love surfing (even though I currently live an appalling distance from the coast—in Kentucky!), and surfing is all about catching good waves. But finding good waves can be tricky. They are the product of a delicate interplay between swell direction, size, period (the distance between waves), tide, wind, shifting sandbars, and more. So a dedicated surfer constantly refines a mental map of where he or she will find the best and least crowded waves. For the region I grew up surfing in Northern California, the mental map readings sound something like this: A 10-foot northwest swell that's washing out a northern pointbreak will be perfect for the inside section of a certain spot in town once the tide drops. And a negative low tide will drain the life out of the points on the east side, but it will awaken that fluky little reef around the corner. The payoff, of course, is good surf. Though the hunt is part of the fun, too.

Maps serve a very practical purpose: they help you get where you want to go. In fact, if you've got a good map and a sense of direction, you will basically never get lost. As I'll occasionally remind my wife when a minor uncertainty arises concerning driving directions, I may not know what to do next, but I'm not lost—I know exactly where I am. (The Jamieson men are renowned, at least among ourselves, for our sense of direction.)

That's one reason why I stubbornly refuse to use a GPS. It's a useful tool in its place, but it's no substitute for a map and a sense of direction. A map gives you the whole picture. It enables you to see far beyond the next freeway exit. And the very act of using a map helps you to make sense of where you are. But when you rely on a GPS, you're wholly at the mercy of some disembodied voice named Stella telling you in her pseudo-British accent that, because of that last turn you just missed, she will now spend the next several minutes "recalculating" while you barrel blindly down the freeway. A map, on the other hand, tells you not just where to go, but where you are.

SOUND DOCTRINE IS GOD'S ROAD MAP FOR THE CHRISTIAN LIFE

Now the point in what I am saying is this: God has given us a road map for living the Christian life, and that map is sound doctrine.

In an ultimate sense, the Bible itself is our map—and the lamp for our feet and light for our path (Ps. 119:105). But sound doctrine simply sums up the message of the Bible. It synthesizes whatever Scripture has to say about any given topic, whether that topic arises from Scripture or from life in the world. It's like what English teachers sometimes say about new vocabulary words: you don't know what a word means unless you can define it in your own words. You cannot just define a word with the same word. Doctrine is like this—it's putting the Bible's teaching on a particular topic in our own words. And doctrine is *sound* whenever our own words summarize the content of the Bible rightly or faithfully, like getting an A+ on a vocabulary quiz. In English class, you get an A+ whenever your words rightly or soundly reproduce the meaning of the vocabulary words.

So how exactly should we define "sound doctrine"? Here's a working definition: *Sound doctrine is a summary of the Bible's teaching that is both faithful to the Bible and useful for life.* Doctrine should not consist of imposing our ideas on the Bible. Rather, it should be nothing more or less than a summary of what the Bible says on a topic. It presents the teaching of

17

Scripture as a coherent though complex unity, which is why I have called it a map. It relates the whole to the parts and the parts to the whole.

Like any good map, then, sound doctrine serves a very useful and practical purpose: sound doctrine is for life. Instruction is for action. We listen to the teaching of God's Word for the purpose of living it out. Sound doctrine isn't an information archive that serves only to present facts. Rather, it's a road map for our pilgrimage from this world to the world to come.

Doctors have to make complicated decisions on short notice with a lot at stake. What enables a good physician to make wise choices is an extensive knowledge of the human body. You can't know if a kidney's failing unless you know what a kidney is and how it should work. That's why doctors spend many years studying human anatomy and physiology so that they can make accurate diagnoses and prescribe appropriate remedies—sometimes with life-saving consequences.

In some ways, the Christian life isn't all that different. We have to make complicated decisions in real time, sometimes with a lot at stake. And, as in practicing medicine, there is no easy formula for some of those decisions, so we need wisdom. The foundations for that wisdom, like the foundations of a doctor's good judgment, lie in a bedrock of knowledge—knowledge of the things God has revealed in his Word. In Scripture, God tells us about who he is, who we are, where we've come from, what's wrong with this world, how God is fixing it, and more. If we're going to live lives that please God, these are the things we most need to know.

Scripture is not exhaustive—there are plenty of true things Scripture *doesn't* say. But it is sufficient. In his Word, God tells us everything we need to know to be saved and to live a life that is pleasing to him (2 Pet. 1:3). Scripture doesn't tell us how to perform heart surgery, but it does lay bare the desires and deceits of all human hearts (Heb. 4:12–13). Scripture doesn't tell us how to get from London to Tokyo, but it does tell us how to walk wisely in the way of the Lord and avoid the snares of the devil (Col. 4:5; 2 Tim. 2:26).

Scripture itself teaches us that sound doctrine is for life. In Titus 2:1, Paul instructs his colaborer, "But as for you, teach what accords with sound doctrine." Then in the next nine verses he describes how different groups of people in the church should live and relate to each other:

- Older men should be sober-minded, self-controlled, sound in faith (v. 2).
- Older women must be reverent, not slanderers or drunkards, and they must teach younger women to be faithful wives and mothers (vv. 3–5).
- Younger men should be self-controlled (v. 6).
- Slaves or workers should submit to their masters and have integrity in their work "so that in everything they may adorn the doctrine of God our Savior" (vv. 9–10).

Note that in verse 1 Paul doesn't command Titus to teach "sound doctrine," though he does insist on that elsewhere in the letter (Titus 1:11; 2:7–8). Instead, Paul commands Titus to teach what "accords with" sound doctrine—what fits with it and flows from it. Titus is to teach the church in Crete to walk in the path that sound doctrine marks out. Their lives are to color in the outlines that sound doctrine provides.

Similarly, in 1 Timothy 1:3–5 Paul writes,

> As I urged you when I was going to Macedonia, remain at Ephesus so that you may charge certain persons not to teach any different doctrine, nor to devote themselves to myths and endless genealogies, which promote speculations rather than the stewardship from God that is by faith. The aim of our charge is love that issues from a pure heart and a good conscience and a sincere faith.

Paul left Timothy in Ephesus so that Timothy would refute those who were preaching false doctrine (v. 3). These false teachings were promoting speculations rather than the stewardship—a rightly ordered life—from God that is by faith (v. 4). For what purpose did Paul give Timothy this charge? So that the Christians in Ephesus would embody the love that flows from a pure heart, good conscience, and sincere faith (v. 5). Sound doctrine leads to sound faith, sound hearts, and sound consciences. And these become the fountain from which flows an entire life that is pleasing to God. The aim of sound doctrine is sound living. As one Christian put it over four hundred years ago, "Theology is the science of living blessedly forever."[1]

Sound doctrine is God's road map for living faithfully in the world. Sound doctrine tells you not just where you are, but who you are, and who God is, and how God has saved us from

---

[1] William Perkins, *The Golden Chain* (1592), in *The Work of William Perkins*, ed. Ian Breward (Appleford: Sutton Courtenay Press, 1990), 177.

sin and enabled us to live lives that are pleasing to him. Sound doctrine is essential equipment for navigating the twisting city streets of our lives. So don't leave home without it.

SOUND DOCTRINE IS FOR LIFE—LIFE *IN* THE CHURCH

When I was a kid, I played basketball, baseball, and soccer for several years. I enjoyed them all well enough, even though I was thoroughly mediocre at each. My favorite sport, if you can call it that, should come as no surprise: surfing.

Surfing is great fun to share with others, especially friends and family, but the act itself is fundamentally individual. A person sits on a board, paddles into a wave, stands up, rides it toward the shore, and then repeats that sequence for as long as one's arms can hold out. Seeing others catch good waves—or, dearer to the heart of most surfers, having others see you—certainly adds to the experience. But that hardly makes it a team sport.

Sports like basketball or football, on the other hand, are inherently corporate. Money and adulation might be lavished on a favorite shooting guard or star quarterback, but the game is played together. It's won or lost together. There's no such thing as a one-man team.

I bring this up because I think most American Christians treat their Christianity more like surfing than like football. We think of our walk with the Lord as something fundamentally individual: I pray. I read the Bible. I attend a worship service to experience God and grow in knowledge of Scripture. I love my neighbor. I share the gospel with others. Sure, it helps to go to church and have Christian friends. But what struc-

tures our priorities, what defines the shape of our discipleship, what serves as our decision-making grid is, most often,
just me and Jesus.

But Scripture teaches that Christianity is much more like
a team sport. It is true that each of us must turn from sin and
trust in Christ in order to be saved (Rom. 10:9–10). Each of us
will give an account of ourselves to God (Rom. 14:10). Each of
us is responsible for what we do (Gal. 6:5). However, unlike
surfing, the very nature of the Christian life is corporate.

- To become a Christian is to be added to the church (Acts
  2:41).
- To get baptized is to be baptized into the body of Christ
  (1 Cor. 12:13).
- To come to faith in Christ is to be brought near, not just to
  God, but to God's people (Eph. 2:17–22).
- To call on and obey God as Father is to have Christians for
  your brothers and sisters (Matt. 12:46–50).

And growth as a Christian is consistently defined in corporate
terms. How many of the fruits of the Spirit (Gal. 5:22–23) can
you practice alone on a desert island?

Consider how Paul describes Christian growth in Ephesians 4:11–16. Christ gives gifts of leaders to his church to
equip the saints for the work of ministry (vv. 11–12) "until
we all attain to the unity of the faith and of the knowledge
of the Son of God, to mature manhood" (v. 13). We speak the
truth in love to one another (v. 15) so that we grow up into
Christ "from whom the whole body, joined and held together
by every joint with which it is equipped, when each part is

working properly, makes the body grow so that it builds itself up in love" (v. 16).

Do you see how closely Paul intertwines the individual Christian's growth and the church's growth? The primary way that we mature as Christians is through the life of the church. The members help the body grow, which means helping each other grow. We are built up as we build others up. Christian growth is a team effort. But Christians are far more than a team—we're members of the same body.

Another passage that unpacks the church's life as a body is 1 Corinthians 12.

- As members of the same body, we can't separate ourselves from the body, as if the body doesn't need us: "If the foot should say, 'Because I am not a hand, I do not belong to the body,' that would not make it any less a part of the body" (v. 15).
- As members of the same body, we can't live autonomously, independent of the other members: "The eye cannot say to the hand, 'I have no need of you'" (v. 21).
- As members of the same body, we must care for all the other members: "But God has so composed the body, giving greater honor to the part that lacked it, that there may be no division in the body, but that the members may have the same care for one another" (vv. 24–25).
- As members of the same body, our lives are tightly interwoven. We rejoice with those who rejoice and weep with those who weep: "If one member suffers, all suffer together; if one member is honored, all rejoice together" (v. 26).

While the "body" metaphor also applies to the universal

23

church, what Paul has in mind here is Christians' participation in a specific local assembly. This is where we suffer or rejoice together, show honor to one another, and interact with members who are radically different from us. This is where we show God's wisdom in composing the body not of one member, but of many (1 Cor. 12:14).

As a member of the body of Christ, your life in a local church should structure your priorities, define the shape of your discipleship, and serve as one of the main grids through which you make many decisions. What it looks like for you to live as a Christian day in and day out should be defined in large part by the life of your local church.[2]

This means that the godly life which flows from sound doctrine is not merely an individual matter. Rather, sound doctrine is for life in the church.

We see this clearly in Romans 12, where Paul appeals to us "by the mercies of God" to live new lives in light of the gospel. After spending eleven chapters expounding the gospel and the doctrines that surround it ("the mercies of God"), Paul shows us that the gospel he preaches has nearly infinite implications for daily living.

What are some of them? First, the gospel and the doctrines that connect to it lead us to devote our lives totally to God, and to be transformed by the ongoing renewal of our minds (Rom. 12:1–2). The gospel calls us to be conformed to God's mind, will, and ways—not the world's. But immediately

---

[2] If you'd like to think more about why it is important for every Christian to be a member of a local church, check out Jonathan Leeman's book *Church Membership: How the World Knows Who Represents Jesus* (Wheaton, IL: Crossway, 2012), also in the 9Marks: Building Healthy Churches series.

after this, Paul tells us not to think of ourselves more highly than we ought (v. 3), but instead to use our gifts to build up the body (vv. 4–8). The gospel teaches us to put others before ourselves, and to use the strengths God has given us to edify our fellow church members—both of which are impossible to do in blissful solitude. Then, in verses 9 through 13, Paul fleshes out more specifics about how we are to love one another, honor one another, and care for each other's needs. When Paul specifies what it means to live in view of God's mercies, he turns immediately to life in the body of Christ.

How can you live in view of God's mercies? By loving and building up the body of Christ. The life that sound doctrine lays out for you is shaped like your local church.

Sound doctrine is for life—life in the church.

SOUND DOCTRINE IS FOR LIFE—THE LIFE *OF* THE CHURCH

If sound doctrine is for life in the church, it's also for the life *of* the church.

Think about the life of a family. What kinds of things would you look at in order to describe it? Here's what you wouldn't do: you wouldn't simply record what each individual family member does throughout the day and then slice and dice your observations into a composite whole. Instead, you'd look at what the family does together. Do they eat together? What do they talk about? Who does the talking? When do they spend time together? What do they do? What are the rules, traditions, customs, and so on that shape how they live together?

The life of a church is similar: what a church does together defines the life of a church. And a church's way of teaching and worshiping and praying and so on deeply impacts every member of the church—just like the culture of a family indelibly stamps every member of the family.

The life of the church is displayed most fully in its corporate worship gatherings. But it's also useful to think about other times members of the church come together. Church members gather outside the main weekly gathering for things like additional teaching, outreach, accountability, and meals in each other's homes.

One of the main arguments I'll be making throughout this book is this: just as sound doctrine is crucial for life, and specifically life in the church, so it is also essential for the life of the church. Like a good map, sound doctrine is eminently useful, so churches should use it.

So in chapters 3 through 6, we'll see how sound doctrine should flow through the whole life of a church and nourish holiness, love, unity, worship, and witness. First, though, we'll look at the fountain itself: how does sound doctrine impact reading and teaching the Bible?

2

SOUND DOCTRINE IS FOR READING AND TEACHING THE BIBLE

"You gotta go to this concert tonight. The greatest saxophonist in the world is playing!" So said my saxophone teacher about an upcoming Michael Brecker concert at Cal State Hayward.

I was in sixth grade and had just begun playing the saxophone the year before. I was quickly developing a love for jazz music through listening to some of my dad's old tapes and CDs of greats like John Coltrane, Thelonious Monk, and Dexter Gordon, but I had never been to a live jazz concert. This would be my first.

"Greatest" is often a disputable title, but Brecker certainly was the premier jazz saxophone virtuoso of his generation. (In 2007, at only fifty-seven years old, Brecker died of leukemia.) That night, rotating between fronting a big band, leading a smaller combo, and playing solo, Michael Brecker transported me into another realm.

While Brecker played, his vintage Selmer Mark VI saxophone seemed less an inanimate hunk of metal than a wizard's wand, able to conjure up any sound he wanted. He could summon a flood of notes out of thin air and cast them perfectly into place faster than any listener could follow. Hearing him improvise was like watching a Rembrandt painting materialize out of thin air: all that perfectly shaded light and dark, all those delicate, invisible brushstrokes, made up as he went, with not a note out of place. But his playing wasn't mere pyrotechnics—it pulsed with focused, fluid emotion as he ranged freely between laughs and cries, laments and lullabies.

It seemed impossible to do what he did with a saxophone, and all the more so because he was making it up as he went. The only word for it was "magic." Indeed, all good improvisation has something magical about it. It's seemingly effortless yet dizzyingly complex. It's spontaneous to its core, yet every note sounds inevitable.

No merely technical description can capture the magic of a live performance by Michael Brecker or any other jazz master, but that doesn't mean there is no technical work going on behind the curtain. On the contrary, Michael Brecker, like virtually every other jazz great, was a relentless practicer. He relished his breaks from the road so that he could spend upwards of eight hours a day working on his technique and vocabulary. In order to be a great jazz improviser, you have to attain a kind of effortless mastery over a wide range of terrain: your instrument's sound and technical demands, the complex logic of jazz harmony, hundreds of tunes and chord progressions, a number of styles and their hybrid offspring, the riffs, clichés, inflections, intonations, and more, which constitute jazz's vocabulary—and the list goes on.

There's more to the magic than the machinery behind the curtain, but without it, there's no magic.

THE "MAGIC" OF A MATURE CHRISTIAN AND THE MACHINERY BEHIND THE CURTAIN

There's also something seemingly magic about the life of a mature Christian. While far from perfect, the life of a mature Christian commands respect and attention, even while similarly defying technical explanation. A mature Christian can bear afflictions with joy, can turn a person from sin with a few well-placed words, can create harmony where conflict abounds.

And, as with a great jazz improviser, there's a lot going on behind the curtain. Among other things, a mature Christian works on mastering—or better, being mastered by—the Bible. He knows how to put it together. He knows how to summarize it and put it in his own words. He knows, in other words, sound doctrine. Remember how we defined sound doctrine in the last chapter? It's a summary of the Bible's teaching that is both faithful to the Bible and useful for life. A godly person will know how to do this. Even if he wouldn't dream of teaching a class full of systematic theology students, a godly person knows what God says about himself and about us in the Bible.

This should come as no surprise, since Scripture itself teaches that it is able to equip us for every good work (2 Tim. 3:16–17). And it teaches that spiritual transformation comes through the renewing of our minds (Rom. 12:1–2), which happens as we soak ourselves in Scripture.

So every Christian has a vested interest in learning to read and teach the Bible wisely. We do this through personal study, but also, perhaps more foundationally, through the church's public proclamation and teaching. This chapter is about how sound doctrine helps us to read and teach the Bible wisely, both personally and in the corporate life of the church.

SOUND DOCTRINE: THE PINS AND BUMPERS OF BIBLE READING

Ultimately, the goal of reading and teaching Scripture is to love God and our neighbor better. And the way to love God more is to know God more. It's true that a person can learn theological facts about God without loving him. At the same time, you cannot love God without knowing him. And to know God, you have to know things *about* him. If you love your wife, you'll want to know about what she's like, what she loves and hates, her past, her plans for the future, and much more.[1] In the same way, we who profess to love God should learn all we can about him.

That's why sound doctrine is an important goal of Bible reading. Sound doctrine summarizes and synthesizes the Bible's teaching into a coherent whole. It tells us what God is like, what he loves and hates, what he's done in the past, and what his plans are for the future. Letting your knowledge of God be determined by one or two isolated passages would be like letting one or two isolated conversations determine your knowledge of your spouse.

Sound doctrine is also an important guardrail for Bible

---

[1] Michael Horton, *The Christian Faith: A Systematic Theology for Pilgrims on the Way* (Grand Rapids, MI: Zondervan, 2011), 13.

reading. It keeps us from wrongly inferring things about God from Scripture that are untrue. In order to interpret Scripture rightly, we need to bring to the table what we already know about God from Scripture—that is, sound doctrine.

To borrow an image from bowling, sound doctrine is both the pins our Bible reading aims at and the bumpers that keep us from rolling into the gutters of error. Sound doctrine helps to send our Scripture reading in the right direction, and it helps keep us rolling in that direction. Sound doctrine is for reading and teaching the Bible.

WHAT IS THE BIBLE? A STORY THAT PREACHES A MESSAGE

In order to unpack in more detail how sound doctrine impacts reading and teaching the Bible, let's first consider what the Bible is.

Is the Bible a magic book you open at random for in-the-moment spiritual guidance? (Anyone for a game of Bible roulette?) Is it an archive of Hallmark cards that gives you an inspirational thought for every season of life? A set of prescriptions for moral self-improvement? An anthology of inspiring myths?

(1) *The Bible is revelation*. God reveals himself to us in his Word. Every single word of Scripture is breathed out by him (2 Tim. 3:16). The authors of Scripture were from different cultures and had different personalities, and they wrote in different genres at different times, but they were all carried along by the Holy Spirit so that they "spoke from God" (2 Pet. 1:21). They all wrote the very words of God.

(2) *The Bible is a story that preaches a message.* From beginning to end, the Bible tells a single story of salvation. From creation, through our fall into sin, to Jesus's saving work on the cross and the eventual restoration of God's rule over all creation, the Bible tells a single epic narrative that spans Genesis to Revelation. It tells the story of how God is working out salvation for his people through his Son Jesus.

Yet this isn't just a story—it's a story that really happened. And it's the story in which we live. We Christians can and must plot our lives on the timeline of the Bible's story: we live after Jesus's death, resurrection, and ascension into heaven, and after the outpouring of the Holy Spirit, but before Jesus's final return. The Bible's story explains where we've come from, where we are, who we are, and where we're going.

Notice how sound doctrine arises from this story and is an integral part of it.

- From creation we learn that God is powerful, and holy, and wise, and good (Psalm 104).
- From the fall we learn that God is perfectly just and his anger burns against sin, yet he is also merciful and patient with sinners, which all of us are (Genesis 3).
- In the life of Jesus we see God's holy and merciful character perfectly displayed (John 1:18; 14:9).
- In the death of Jesus we see God's justice and love working together to accomplish salvation (Rom. 3:21–26; 5:6–11).
- In Jesus's resurrection we see the victory over death that God promises to all his people (2 Cor. 4:14).
- In Jesus's promise to return and restore God's rule over all of creation we see God's faithfulness, his lavish generosity toward his people, and more (Rev. 22:12).

32

In other words, the Bible is a story that preaches a message. To borrow Michael Horton's phrase, it's a drama that gives rise to dogma. It's a narrative that's full of teaching. Sound doctrine arises from the Bible's grand story of salvation.[2]

(3) *The Bible is an instrument in God's hand to carry out his redeeming work.* When we read Scripture, we are confronted by the voice of the living God (Heb. 4:12–13). And God's Word is invincibly powerful—it never fails to accomplish his purposes (Isa. 55:10–11). Those purposes include saving sinners and sanctifying those who are in Christ (1 Pet. 1:23–25; John 17:17; 1 Thess. 2:13). So, when we come to Scripture, we should expect to be changed by it. We should expect it to push us further down the path of our pilgrimage. We should expect it to shape us more fully into the image of Christ.

Because the Bible is a story that preaches a message, we should pay attention to both the story and the message, even though we should never draw too hard a line between these two things. Let's consider each in turn.

HOW TO READ THE BIBLE AS A SINGLE STORY

Scripture does tell a unified story from beginning to end, but putting that story together isn't as simple as reading straight through from Genesis to Revelation. (Just ask someone who has tried that and thrown in the towel once they hit Leviticus.) Therefore, it's important to develop the skill of discerning how any passage of Scripture fits into the larger story.

Here are several steps that should help toward that end:

---

[2] If you want to think about this in more detail, see Michael Horton's discussion in *The Christian Faith*, 19, 27–30.

(1) *Read through all of the Old Testament.* If you can, read whole books in a short span, in one sitting if possible. That helps you keep the big picture in view. Learn the overall history of Israel from the patriarchs to the return from exile. As you read, pay special attention to the covenants God makes with Noah (Gen. 8:20–9:17), Abraham (Gen. 12:1–3; 15:1–21), the nation of Israel (Exodus 19–24), and David (2 Sam. 7:1–17), and especially the new covenant God promises through Jeremiah (Jer. 31:31–34). Each covenant adds something to the unfolding of God's purposes in creation and redemption.

(2) *Read and reread all four Gospels.* Each of the Gospels presents a rich theological portrait of Jesus as the fulfillment of all of God's Old Testament promises. So pay attention to connections the Gospel authors make between Jesus and the Old Testament. Further, notice how the Gospels continue the Old Testament's story of God's saving acts by revealing the hinge of the entire story: the life, death, and resurrection of Jesus.

(3) *Pay special attention whenever a New Testament author quotes or alludes to an Old Testament passage.* Jesus himself taught the apostles how to interpret the Old Testament rightly—that is, in light of his death and resurrection (Luke 24:27, 44–47). So let the apostles be your guides to connecting the dots between the Testaments.

(4) *Carefully study places where the biblical authors themselves put together pieces of the whole story of Scripture.* Stephen's speech in Acts 7 is one place. Paul's sermon in Acts 13:16–41 is another: here Paul unpacks how Jesus's life,

death, and resurrection fulfill "what God promised to the fathers" (v. 32). In Galatians 3–4, Paul explains how the gospel both fulfills God's promise to Abraham and ends the era of the law of Moses. In Hebrews, especially chapters 8–10, the author explains how Jesus's death is a perfect, once-for-all fulfillment of the Old Testament's sacrificial system. The result is that now, through the death of Christ, believers have forgiveness of sins, new hearts, and free access to God—and the old system is finished forever. Passages like these help us to make sense out of the Old Testament in the first place. They also show us how the work of Christ fulfills, completes, and sometimes does away with what has come before in the story of salvation.

The goal in all this is to understand the Bible's single, unified story. Sometimes theologians call this kind of reading "biblical theology"—theology that traces out the development of the progressively unfolding revelation of God in Scripture.[3]

It's important to learn to read Scripture this way in order to rightly interpret it and apply it to our lives. Understanding where a passage falls within the overall story goes a long way toward relating it to the place in the story that we occupy. Here are just a couple examples:

- As Christians, the purity regulations of Leviticus aren't binding on us—Christ has fulfilled and thereby abolished them. But they still reveal God's holiness to us, and his demand that we be holy (Lev. 19:2).

---

[3] For more on biblical theology, see Michael Lawrence's *Biblical Theology in the Life of the Church: A Guide for Ministry* (Wheaton, IL: Crossway, 2010).

- Joshua's conquest of Canaan is neither a model for foreign policy nor an example of ancient barbarism. Instead, it was a divinely mandated act of judgment. In this specific instance, God's end-time judgment of sin was brought forward into the present (Gen. 15:16).

Viewing Scripture as a single story is one of the most important lenses for reading it rightly, and it brings some of the greatest rewards. It enables us to climb to the peaks of the revelation of God's saving acts and catch a view of the epic that stretches before us from eternity past into eternity future.

HOW TO READ THE BIBLE FOR ITS MESSAGE

But Scripture is not merely a story, it's a story that preaches a message. That message is the good news that Jesus has died on the cross and risen from the grave in order to satisfy God's wrath and bring salvation to all those who turn from their sin and trust in him. But like a sprawling, aged tree that sends its roots out far and wide, the basic message of the gospel also connects with virtually every other topic the Bible addresses.

For example, God's character matters for how we live. When your life seems out of control, it matters that God is utterly sovereign (Eph. 1:11; Rom. 8:28; Amos 3:6). When you're going through a painful trial, it matters that God is good (Ps. 106:1). When you're burdened by sin, it matters that God is merciful and gracious, slow to anger and abounding in steadfast love, and that he promises to forgive our sin (Ex. 34:6; 1 John 1:9). Every facet of the Bible's teaching is relevant for how we live, whether that teaching is about the character of God, the acts of God, the nature of humanity, the world we inhabit, God's plan for the future, or anything else.

So how do you read the Bible for its message?

(1) *Begin with the conviction that Scripture is the Word of God.* It is the revelation of God himself. Therefore, Scripture is our sole supreme authority concerning everything it speaks to. Because God is totally truthful (Titus 1:2), everything he says is trustworthy and true (Ps. 12:6). Because Scripture is a revelation of the mind of God, Scripture's teaching is coherent—it hangs together as a whole. This means that, properly interpreted, Scripture never contradicts itself, and it never misleads us in any way. Because Scripture is God's Word, it has a coherent message, and that message is authoritative for us.

(2) *Read and reread the whole story, carefully discerning the meaning that arises from the story itself.* Just as you should read a whole book before making definitive judgments about it, so you should always be engaging the Scriptures to learn more about what God has revealed of himself. And the better you understand the Scriptures themselves, the better you'll grasp the message they proclaim.

(3) *Allow Scripture to interpret Scripture.* Scripture doesn't contradict itself, so allow the clearer portions to aid you in interpreting the less clear. When something confusing comes up, search out other passages of Scripture that address the same issue and see if you can begin to make sense of the whole.

(4) *As you grow in true knowledge of God through Scripture, that knowledge becomes part of the lens through which you continue to read Scripture.* That's part of how you continually spi-

ral into a deeper, richer, more accurate reading of the Bible. For example, Scripture declares beyond a shadow of a doubt that Jesus Christ is fully God and fully man (John 1:1, 14). So, if you come to a passage that seems to call one of those doctrines into question, interpret that passage in light of what you have already been convinced of.

(5) *Continually draw connections between the parts and the whole.* Scripture doesn't reveal isolated doctrines to us; it reveals the very character of God. So consider how God's attributes fit together. His love and justice, his mercy and holiness—these don't contradict each other, but work together in harmony.

Because Scripture faithfully represents the mind of God, the teaching of Scripture can be put together into a coherent whole. We can sum up what Scripture as a whole says about its central concerns, such as the character of God, the state of creation, the nature and fallenness of man, the saving work of Christ, the life of the church, and the promise of the world to come. Working through these topics in an orderly progression is often called "systematic theology."

Although there's not a one-to-one correspondence, what we mean by "sound doctrine" throughout this book has a lot to do with systematic theology, as well as with biblical theology. It embraces both, with an accent on the former, since systematic theology is a way of reading the Bible that summarizes and synthesizes the teachings of Scripture and brings them to bear on our lives.[4]

---

[4] If you're looking for a readable and devotional introduction to systematic theology, check out Wayne Grudem's *Systematic Theology: An Introduction to Christian Doctrine,* 2nd ed. (Grand Rapids, MI: Zondervan, 2007).

(6) *Consider how Scripture speaks to whatever issues you're facing in life, such as marriage, or money, or work, or friendship.* When we read Scripture carefully and keep the whole story in mind, we can synthesize its teachings and apply them to situations beyond what the biblical authors experienced or envisioned. Obviously, none of these topics is the main point of the Bible, but Scripture speaks coherently and powerfully, if sometimes indirectly, to all of life. "What does this mean to me?" isn't the first question we should ask when we open up the Bible, but it is a question we should always arrive at. Systematic theology helps us to put together the teaching of the Bible as a whole, which is another crucial step in applying the Bible to our lives. Seeing how any given passage fits with other teachings of Scripture is an important part of rightly bringing the Bible to bear on our daily lives.

Scripture is a story that preaches a message. And the goal of reading and teaching Scripture is to be conformed to the image of Christ. Putting the story together and getting the message right are key components to the machinery behind the curtain of a godly Christian life.

BIG-PICTURE BENEFITS OF SOUND DOCTRINE

With that in mind, let's think a little more about the benefits of sound doctrine for reading and teaching the Bible.

The first big-picture benefit of sound doctrine is that, well, it provides the big picture, and the big picture helps us understand all the details of Scripture. Imagine a small geographic area, no bigger than a few square miles, which contains an unusual concentration of large, vicious, predatory animals. This unusually populated region, it turns out, is very close to the heart of a major metropolitan center. Not only that, but the locals allow their children to roam freely inside this region—it's even considered a form of entertainment!

Now, if I told you that this "small geographic area" is the Louisville Zoo (if you guessed "a zoo," go to the head of the class), all of those details would suddenly make sense—and you would see each of them in a very different light.

The point is that having the big picture up front helps you to see how all the details fit in. It helps to shine light on what could otherwise remain dark. And sound doctrine gives us the big picture: a wide-angle view of who God is, who we are, and how God is working out salvation for those who trust in Christ.

Another big-picture benefit of sound doctrine is that it acts like a minesweeper. A balanced diet of sound doctrine can expose and defuse our unbiblical thoughts and attitudes that would otherwise go undetected. Because of sin, we all have wrong ideas about God. Sometimes those wrong ideas can go unchallenged for years, even decades. But teaching that presents "the whole counsel of God" (Acts 20:27) revealed in Scripture prompts us to deal with those errors. It takes us by the hand and points out biblical passages that overthrow cherished convictions we've picked up not from Scripture but from our culture. Sound doctrine exposes the ways we've tried to make God in our own image, rather than heeding his gracious revelation about the way things really are.

Similarly, sound doctrine helps to expose our blind spots and correct our imbalances. Whether by culture, disposition, church tradition, or other factors, we're all prone to emphasize certain aspects of the Bible's teaching to the neglect or even denial of others. The ballast of biblical doctrine helps set the ship right. It enables us to understand the Bible's teaching in its fullness and balance, rather than simply clutching at the parts we like best. Further, a full-orbed view of sound doctrine sensitizes us to the things we tend to screen out, or simply not notice, when we study Scripture. It helps to correct our vision, so that we can truly see what God has revealed of himself in his Word.

Further, sound doctrine helps us map the Bible onto our lives. Sound doctrine reminds us that God's story of salvation is the story we're actually living in. It gives us clear vision to see the world as it really is—that is, as God says it is. And so sound doctrine helps us to practically apply the Bible. Too often we have neat little divisions between "religion" and "real life." We seal the Bible off from our daily lives, as if it somehow only applies to the things we do for an hour on Sunday morning. But sound doctrine gives us a cohesive, all-encompassing way of looking at the world. When we grasp this, the Bible is no longer merely a book of wisdom for specifically religious needs, but the lens through which we make sense of everything in our lives.

Finally, sound doctrine is a guard against false teaching. Not every so-called Bible teacher actually teaches the Bible. Many preachers grievously mishandle the Word of God. Scripture plainly says that false teachers will always be a threat to the church (Acts 20:29–31; Eph. 4:14). And the best way to discover a counterfeit is to know the genuine article like the back of your hand.

Sadly, false teachers will always gain a hearing because they say what we want to hear (2 Tim. 4:3–4). The best antidote to an appetite for false teaching is a steady diet of sound doctrine. The best way to prevent doctrinal disease is a regular regimen of the preventive medicine of scriptural theology.

SOUND DOCTRINE IS FOR READING AND TEACHING THE BIBLE IN THE CHURCH

How then should sound doctrine influence how the Bible is read and taught in the church? Here I have four main points, all aimed at pastors, though they're the kind of thing that every Christian should be aware of.

First, the main point of the church's weekly assembly is to edify believers (1 Cor. 14:12, 14, 26). Therefore, use that time to instruct your people in sound doctrine. Expositional preaching—preaching that takes the main point of a biblical text, makes that the main point of the sermon, and applies it to the life of the church—should constitute the bulk of a church's preaching diet.[5] But your sermons shouldn't give the impression that each text exists in a vacuum. Rather, without turning every sermon into a doctrinal treatise, each sermon should in some way help your people connect the dots between the sermon text and the rest of Scripture. This doesn't mean you need to discuss lots of other Scripture pas-

---

[5] For an explanation and defense of this idea, see chapter 5 of Jonathan Leeman's book *Reverberation: How God's Word Brings Light, Freedom, and Action to His People* (Chicago: Moody, 2011).

sages, but it does require you to preach with the big picture in view. Also, the rest of the service—singing, prayers, and more—should be shot through with sound doctrine. We'll think more about the other elements in corporate worship in chapters 3 and 6.

Second, treat the Sunday morning sermon like the main meal that it is, and not as a mere appetizer to entice people into what else the church has to offer. In other words, don't put your congregation on a low-doctrine diet. The Bible is a meaty book, and in order to grow, Christians need lots of calories worth of sound doctrine. So make your sermons doctrine-rich enough to satisfy the appetite of a growing Christian.

Third, if sound doctrine is for life, then theology is for application. Some preachers teach tons of theology with little application. There are worse ways to preach, but it's easy to see how that would lead to Christians who have a lot of knowledge but little know-how, or an abundance of doctrinal precision but a scarcity of love. However, much more common in evangelical preaching today is tons of application with little or no theology. In some ways, that's far worse. If your preaching is all application with no theology, then you simply aren't preaching the gospel. So ground your application in the text and in the theology that arises from the text. Show your people how the indicatives of the gospel lead directly to the imperatives of the Christian life. In your sermons, model for them the glorious truth that the Christian life is a response to what God has already done for us in Christ.

Finally, feed your church a steady diet of sound doctrine in Sunday school classes and other teaching contexts. Use opportunities outside the Sunday service to delve deeper into specific doctrinal subjects than you can profitably manage in a sermon.

We grow as Christians by applying truth to life. So cultivate in your people a hunger for good theology. Give them a regular diet of it and patiently wait as their appetites catch up.

SOUND DOCTRINE IS FOR DOING THEOLOGY IN COMMUNITY

Finally, how should all this filter into every Christian's personal discipleship to Christ?

First, realize that your church's teaching is the primary means God uses to grow your knowledge of him. This doesn't mean that personal study is unimportant. But it does mean that the corporate teaching of the church is most important.

You may be reading Jonah in your quiet times and profiting greatly from it. Personal Bible reading is important, and I don't want to downplay it at all. But if your pastor is preaching through Luke, there are dozens or even hundreds of people in your church being exposed to Luke every week. So take advantage of that. Prepare for sermons by meditating on the text ahead of time. Use the shared teaching you're receiving to fuel conversations with other church members throughout the week. Do theology in community by exploring the sermon's theological and practical repercussions with other church members, and by putting the truth into practice together.

Don't just view the sermon as a one-off event each week. Rather, view it as a fountain that sends a stream of biblical truth into the life of the church. That stream can be directed into a thousand channels that bring biblical and doctrinal nourishment where it's needed—and some of that channeling work should be done by every single member of the church.

Sound doctrine is for reading and teaching the Bible in the church. So allow your church's teaching to drive your growth as a theologian and as a Christian. Take your efforts to grow and disciple others and hitch them to the engine that's driving the whole church: the teaching and preaching of the Word.

THE GOAL OF SOUND DOCTRINE–DRIVEN READING AND TEACHING: MASTERFUL IMPROVISATION

Sound doctrine helps us to read and teach the Bible wisely. When we learn to map the storyline of salvation and tease out the message of Scripture as a whole, we gain essential machinery for progressing in the Christian life. Mastering the Bible is necessary for Christian growth, and sound doctrine is a starting point, guardrail, and goal of reading Scripture rightly.

Of course, the goal in all this is not mere knowledge, but growth in godliness. The purpose of working on our technique as theologians is that we would be able to masterfully improvise in the real-life performance that is the Christian life. In doing theology we're not ultimately seeking facts, but fellowship with God and the fruit of godly lives and healthy churches.

In each of the remaining chapters we're going to explore one of the fruits that sound doctrine causes to grow in the life of the church. First up is one that in some sense encompasses all the rest: holiness.

3

SOUND DOCTRINE
IS FOR HOLINESS

John MacArthur can be a thrilling preacher. That's not because he's a gripping storyteller or he takes you on an emotional rollercoaster. Actually, his preaching style is plain, even a little monotonous.

The first time I heard him preach, I thought it was pretty boring. It was Easter Sunday during my freshman year of college, and I visited Grace Community Church in Sun Valley, California, where MacArthur pastors. He was preaching from 1 Corinthians 15 about how we know Jesus was resurrected. The sermon was full of arguments. It referred to lots of biblical passages. It seemed to go on forever.

In retrospect, maybe it wasn't the most exciting sermon he ever preached, but that's not why I thought it was boring. The main reason was that I didn't have much of an appetite for doctrine. Over the previous couple years, my knowledge of Scripture had been growing, but most of what MacArthur said still flew over my head.

Yet I was intrigued by MacArthur's deep knowledge of the Bible and the certainty of his conviction. I was also impressed by the people I met in his church. They seemed to know the Bible well and to live out their faith more consistently than I did. You could tell from how they talked, how they treated each other, and how they committed themselves to the church.

I had come to the University of Southern California in downtown Los Angeles to study jazz saxophone—yes, you can major in that in college, at least in California. During the first week of class, I got to know a drummer named Jon. He came over to my apartment to borrow Joe Henderson's CD *Page One* (a great album, by the way). When he saw Wayne Grudem's *Systematic Theology* sitting on my shelf—a recent gift from a pastor who had discipled me before I left for college—we instantly hit it off. We were some of the only Christians in our degree program, so we naturally stuck together. Yet Jon was so much godlier than I that he ended up discipling me without even trying. He just had to be himself, and that exposed my sin and showed me what faithfulness looked like. He also kept inviting me to his church.

So when I moved back to L.A. for my sophomore year, I was thinking seriously about plugging my life into Grace Community Church. But what happened on my first Sunday back made the decision to join a no-brainer.

SHINY BALD MAN WITH A SCALPEL

On that Sunday in late August, C. J. Mahaney, then pastor of Covenant Life Church in Maryland, was filling the pulpit for Pastor John. In the morning service he preached on James 4:1–2. I was sitting near the back of Grace Church's

3,500-person worship center, but the sermon was so absorbing that I hardly noticed the football-field distance separating me from the preacher, or the thousands of other people in the room. My main visual memory of the sermon is C. J.'s shiny bald head flashing in the platform's stage lighting as he paced back and forth. But it's what I heard that really mattered.

James 4:1–2 says, "What causes quarrels and what causes fights among you? Is it not this, that your passions are at war within you? You desire and do not have, so you murder. You covet and cannot obtain, so you fight and quarrel. You do not have, because you do not ask." C. J. simply walked through the passage, liberally illustrating James's teaching with negative examples from his own life. His outline went something like this:

- Relational conflict is more serious than you think.
- Relational conflict is simpler than you think.
- Relational conflict is worse than you think.
- And solving relational conflict is easier than you think.

The point of the message was that cravings cause conflicts. Conflicts happen when our sinful desires lead us to use other people to get what we want, rather than serve them in love. The solution is the gospel of Jesus Christ. Instead of blaming circumstances and other people, we need to repent, confess our sins to God, ask others for forgiveness, and remind ourselves of who Jesus is and what he's done for us in his death and resurrection.

This bland summary doesn't do justice to the sermon, but that was the basic idea, and I had never heard anything like it.

It sliced cleanly to the heart of real issues in my life. It was like a scalpel that cut through all my defenses and started doing open-heart surgery.

BLOWING THE DOORS OPEN AND FLIPPING ON THE LIGHTS

At the time I heard that sermon, I had been a Christian for several years, but my growth in Christ had been slow and patchy. I had been in a romantic relationship that was not an asset to my discipleship. The summer leading up to that school year, however, my girlfriend broke up with me because she was sick of me acting like a selfish jerk. Hers was a fair evaluation, though I didn't want to admit it at the time.

But then, right in the middle of that sermon, I had to admit it. I couldn't shrug it off anymore. All of a sudden I could see a hundred "little" conflicts in that relationship and many others in a new light. It was as if dozens of past sins in my life had been locked up in a hallway of dark rooms and now someone was running through the hallway, blowing all the doors open, and flipping on the lights.

That sermon changed me. It gave me a whole new set of eyes to see my life. It exploded all kinds of excuses and rationalizations. It deflated my opinion of myself. And it revealed a path to deeper, more consistent growth as a Christian.

And, like I said, that sermon also made joining Grace Church a no-brainer. I thought, "If this is the kind of guy they get to be a guest preacher, I'd better stick around for the regular program." So I joined the church a few months later and really threw my life into it. And God used the preaching, teaching, and discipling of the pastors and friends like Jon to transform my life from the inside out.

WHAT HAPPENED?

What happened to me during that sermon? Here it is in a nut-shell: God used sound doctrine to produce holiness. It didn't instantaneously make me perfect (if only!), but the sound doctrine in that sermon produced real change in my mind and heart.

James 4:1–2 gave me a doctrinal analysis of interpersonal conflict. It didn't use fancy theological terms, but it gave me a doctrine of man, a doctrine of sin, and a doctrine of sanctification. Why do conflicts happen? Ultimately conflict arises from wicked desires, not incompatible personalities or unfortunate circumstances. And what's the solution? Repentance and faith.

I had been able to shrug off criticism because I wasn't looking at myself through this biblical lens. But C. J. handed me this doctrinal lens and, by God's grace and the enabling of the Holy Spirit, I was able to see myself in a new, uglier, and more accurate light. And that brought real change.

SOUND DOCTRINE IS FOR HOLINESS

In order to grow in holiness, it is crucial that you understand the biblical doctrine of sin and view your life through that lens. If you don't know what your problem is, you won't know what to do about it. Every biblical doctrine, embraced by the mind and applied to the heart, conforms us to the character and will of God. Sound doctrine drives us to devote ourselves more completely to God in our thoughts, desires, attitudes, words, and actions—which is what the Bible calls "holiness."

This holiness takes a thousand concrete forms in our lives. C. J.'s sermon, for example, helped me to become more holy in my speech and how I related to others, especially in dealing with conflict.

Sound doctrine is a central means by which Christians grow in holiness, and holiness is the goal of sound doctrine. As we saw in chapter 1, sound doctrine is a summary of the Bible's teaching that is both faithful to the Bible and useful for life. And, as Paul says to Timothy, "All Scripture is breathed out by God and profitable for teaching, for reproof, for correction, and for training in righteousness, that the man of God may be complete, equipped for every good work" (2 Tim. 3:16–17). Did you catch that? All Scripture is profitable for training in righteousness. Training in righteousness is exactly what we need. It's certainly what I need. And if you understand the Bible's doctrine of sin, you know that you need it, too.

As Christians, we've been given new, Spirit-indwelt natures, but sin still lives in us (Rom. 7:17). It still blinds us to ourselves, entices us to do wrong, and corrupts our desires. It still tempts us to worship ourselves rather than God. So we need the high-beams of biblical doctrine to light our road so that we don't veer off into a ditch. We need the sun of a biblical worldview to burn off the fog of sin that clings to our minds and hearts.

Jesus himself teaches us that sound doctrine is for holiness. In John 17, Jesus prays for his disciples in view of his coming death and resurrection:

> But now I am coming to you, and these things I speak in the
> world, that they may have my joy fulfilled in themselves. I have
> given them your word, and the world has hated them because
> they are not of the world, just as I am not of the world. I do not
> ask that you take them out of the world, but that you keep them
> from the evil one. They are not of the world, just as I am not of
> the world. Sanctify them in the truth; your word is truth. As
> you sent me into the world, so I have sent them into the world.
> And for their sake I consecrate myself, that they also may be
> sanctified in truth. (John 17:13–19)

In verse 17, Jesus asks the Father to sanctify us in the truth,
the truth of his Word. To sanctify a person is to separate him
or her from sin and totally devote that person to God's purposes. So Jesus lived a perfectly obedient life and suffered
on the cross as our substitute with the goal that we would be
sanctified in truth—made holy by God's Word (v. 19). He totally devoted himself to God in order that we would be totally
devoted to God. And the instrument God uses to bring about
that total devotion is his Word.

Paul also tells us that sound doctrine is what teaches us to
live rightly. He writes in 1 Timothy,

> Now we know that the law is good, if one uses it lawfully, un-
> derstanding this, that the law is not laid down for the just but
> for the lawless and disobedient, for the ungodly and sinners,
> for the unholy and profane, for those who strike their fathers
> and mothers, for murderers, the sexually immoral, men who
> practice homosexuality, enslavers, liars, perjurers, and what-
> ever else is contrary to sound doctrine, in accordance with the
> gospel of the glory of the blessed God with which I have been
> entrusted. (1 Tim. 1:8–11)

Did you notice what Paul says toward the end of the passage? He says that all of these ungodly actions are "contrary to sound doctrine." Paul sees godly living as a direct implication, even a demand, of sound doctrine.

Sound doctrine is not abstract data. It isn't ideas floating around in space. It's not bare facts, like the fact that right now I'm listening to Bill Evans's album "You Must Believe in Spring" (another good album). No, sound doctrine comes with a practical program, a plan for a new life. Sound doctrine commands sound living.

If we claim to believe sound doctrine but don't love God and our neighbor, then something is wrong—most likely there's a disconnect between head and heart. Sadly, it's all too common for us to let knowledge of God simply dwell in our heads, rather than drilling it into our hearts. When we neglect to work doctrine into our hearts—our emotions, desires, affections, hopes, longings, fears—we're forgetting what doctrine is *for*. We need to plant doctrine deep in our hearts so that the fruit of conformity to Christ may grow up in our lives and churches for God's glory.

In fact, that's exactly what Paul prays in Philippians:

> And it is my prayer that your love may abound more and more, with knowledge and all discernment, so that you may approve what is excellent, and so be pure and blameless for the day of Christ, filled with the fruit of righteousness that comes through Jesus Christ, to the glory and praise of God. (Phil. 1:9–11)

Paul prays that we would grow in knowledge and discernment—that we would agree with, approve, and desire the things that are best. This involves more than sound doctrine, of course, but embracing sound doctrine is where discernment begins.

For what purpose does Paul pray this? In order that we would live righteous lives and so bring God glory. Paul wants us to embrace sound doctrine so that our lives and churches will be filled with the fruit of righteousness and God will be praised. Sound doctrine is for holiness.

DOCTRINES THAT PRODUCE HOLINESS

In this chapter I've recounted how the biblical doctrine of sin helped me grow in holiness. And as we've seen, all Scripture is profitable for training in righteousness. This means that every biblical doctrine works to conform us to the image of Christ.

Consider the doctrine of God. God's holiness, justice, omnipresence, and sovereignty over all things hold infinite implications for what our lives should look like. Think also of God's patience, compassion, and mercy. These aspects of who God is should also spur us on to holiness, which God's character defines. How do we know what it means to be holy? We look to God. Listen to what Peter says:

> As obedient children, do not be conformed to the passions of your former ignorance, but as he who called you is holy, you also be holy in all your conduct, since it is written, "You shall be holy, for I am holy." And if you call on him as Father who judges impartially according to each one's deeds, conduct yourselves with fear throughout the time of your exile. (1 Pet. 1:14–17)

Since God is holy, we are to be holy in everything we do. This means that we must leave behind every passion and every desire that does not match up to our knowledge of God (v. 14). Further, since God judges all people impartially, we are to live before him in reverent fear throughout our lives (v. 17). God is our Father, but he is also the Judge of all. So we must live in light of his absolute justice. And God's justice defines what it means for us to live rightly. As we look to him, we learn how to live. As we learn more about his character, we gain a pattern for our own.

Or consider God's promise to perfectly establish his kingdom when Christ returns—what we call the doctrine of "eschatology," or the last things. Here's what the apostle John says about that certain hope:

> Beloved, we are God's children now, and what we will be has not yet appeared; but we know that when he appears we shall be like him, because we shall see him as he is. And everyone who thus hopes in him purifies himself as he is pure. (1 John 3:2–3)

On the last day, we will be like Christ. We will be perfectly righteous, perfectly conformed to the character of God, just like he is. Therefore, John says, everyone who has this hope purifies himself. Because we will be like Christ on the last day, we want to be like him now, and we work hard toward that end.

Both of these passages make a direct connection between sound doctrine and living holy lives, and there are countless more examples of such connections that we could mine from the Scriptures. All of Scripture is useful for conforming us to the character of Christ. Every biblical doctrine, properly understood and applied, helps bring our minds, hearts, and wills closer to Christ's.

HOW THESE FRUITS GROW

Sound doctrine breeds holiness not only in our lives as individuals, but also in the corporate life of the church. How? Here's a sketch of how sound doctrine helps the fruits of holiness grow through four different aspects of the church's life together:

1. PREACHING AND TEACHING

As we saw in chapter 2, a church's preaching and teaching should be filled with sound doctrine. Doctrine should be the frame that supports the whole edifice of the church's teaching—not always visible, but always giving shape to the whole. And sometimes it should even come onto center stage.

As pastors and other church leaders preach and teach sound doctrine, our minds are gradually conformed to the mind of Christ. Week by week, day by day, we uproot lies and plant truths. As those truths take root in our hearts, they transform our desires, affections, and actions. Just as a healthy diet leads to a sound body, so a diet of sound doctrine in preaching produces holiness in a church's members.

2. SINGING

As we'll consider further in chapter 6, sound doctrine is the fuel of worship. This means that the songs we sing when we gather as churches should burst with sound doctrine. Singing gives a church a chance to rejoice together in truths about who God is. It gives it the opportunity to celebrate together what he's done in salvation. In all this, singing helps to move doctrine from the head to the heart, and to set our hearts aflame.

As we sing truths about God to God, our emotions are made holy. All too often, we rejoice in the wrong things, celebrate the wrong things, delight in the wrong things. Singing sound doctrine helps us to rejoice in, to celebrate, and to delight in the triune God. And this helps our whole character to become more conformed to Christ's.

This is not merely an individual experience, but a corporate one. Paul exhorted the Romans, "May the God of endurance and encouragement grant you to live in such harmony with one another, in accord with Christ Jesus, that together you may with one voice glorify the God and Father of our Lord Jesus Christ" (Rom. 15:5–6). Paul charged the Romans to pursue unity in order to offer unified, harmonious worship to God. But it's also true that worshiping God unites us. When we glorify God with one voice, our hearts are united in holiness. Together, as a church, we become more like Christ as we praise God in song.

3. PRAYER

What we ask of God reveals our hearts' desires. It reveals who we are. That's why we should pray sound doctrine both individually and corporately.

Have you ever noticed how prayers in the Bible are full of

sound doctrine? Consider the prayers of confession in Nehemiah 9 and Daniel 9. Or think about how much doctrine undergirds the Lord's Prayer (Matt. 6:9–13). It begins by affirming God's glory ("Hallowed be your name."). It asks him to fulfill his promises and conform all things to his holy will ("Your kingdom come, your will be done, on earth as it is in heaven."). And it rests on God's sovereignty and provision ("Give us this day our daily bread"). When Jesus taught his disciples to pray, he showed them how to put their doctrine to work.

Our churches, too, should practice employing sound doctrine for the sake of praising God for who he is, thanking him for what he has done, confessing our sin, and asking him for things that we know are pleasing to him. When our churches' prayers are increasingly filled with sound doctrine, they become more holy—and so do we.

4. MODELING

Another venue through which doctrine should produce holiness in the church is modeling. I don't mean striking a pose and taking photos. I mean the Bible's teaching that all Christians should both learn from and serve as godly examples.

Throughout the New Testament, we are told to imitate godly examples. Hebrews tells us, "Remember your leaders, those who spoke to you the word of God. Consider the outcome of their way of life, and imitate their faith" (Heb. 13:7). And Paul writes, "Brothers, join in imitating me, and keep your eyes on those who walk according to the example you have in us" (Phil. 3:17).

As Christians, we should imitate those who are sound in

faith and life. And we should strive to set such an example for others. This is one of the main things that helped me grow as a Christian during my time at Grace Church, and that's still the case for me today.

Sound doctrine is key to this because it is what fuels godliness. When we imitate others or invite others to imitate us, we're not simply playing copycat—monkey see, monkey do. We're not trying simply to replicate specific behaviors. Rather, we're receiving and passing on a right response to sound doctrine. How do you find contentment in the midst of financial difficulty? By cherishing the riches that we have in Christ and that will be revealed on the last day (1 Pet. 1:4–5). How do you trust in the Lord through a severe trial? By leaning hard into God's goodness and sovereignty (Job 1:21).

Sound doctrine is the script for sound living. So a godly example is someone who can say, "I'm living this way because of what God's Word says. Here, look. See for yourself." They can teach you how to live according to this script because they practice it every day. A godly example is someone who can teach you the intricate dance steps of the Christian life because he knows the music by heart.

In all of these aspects of the church's life, sound doctrine is the fuel for spiritual growth. So let's inject that fuel into our churches and daily lives so that we become engines of growth in holiness.

THE POWER AND THRILL OF SOUND DOCTRINE

I may have been bored the first time I heard him, but, as I said, John MacArthur can be a thrilling preacher. Why? For the same reason that every single pastor who preaches the Bible faithfully is a thrilling preacher: God's Word is powerful to transform sinners and conform us to the image of Christ. Sound doctrine has power—power to make us holy. When we listen carefully to what God's Word says about ourselves, God, salvation, and much more, we plug into a power source that's infinitely greater than the grids that keep cities humming.

That power changed my perspective on Grace Community Church from boring to thrilling. That power set off a chain reaction in my life that is still firing today. That power can transform the character of entire churches. And that power will drive all our growth in holiness until we are made perfectly pure, just as he is.

Sound doctrine is for holiness.

4

SOUND DOCTRINE
IS FOR LOVE

Sailing is one of the most enchanting activities I can imagine. I hardly ever get to do it, but when I do, it's like stepping into another world.

One of the best things about sailing is the quiet. There's no motor, only the steady splash-and-hiss of the hull slicing through the waves and an occasional sail flapping when the wind shifts. This quiet is the purposeful stillness of a well-wrought craft greeting the force it was made to embrace. It's the pregnant silence of nature seamlessly translated into wonder: a journey at sea.

A sailboat, of course, doesn't generate its own forward motion. Instead, the size and angle of the sails, the design of the hull, and the shape of the keel down below all work together to enable the sailboat to turn wind into movement.

This means that you have to pay constant attention to the wind. If it drops, you raise a jib to catch more of it. If it comes up fast, you may need to haul in some sail so that you're not overpowered. If it dies, you're stuck.

Sailing makes you utterly dependent on the wind. You

can't go anywhere without it. All your motion is a response to the wind's push. You can't just jump in, turn the key, and zip away. Something much bigger and stronger than your little ship has to fill the sails and push you along.

LOVE, WIND, SAILBOATS, AND SOUND DOCTRINE

People today often think love is like the wind. It blows where it wills. You can't control it. You can't *do* anything about it. If you're in love with your spouse, great. But if you wake up one morning "out of love," go ahead and get a divorce.

Or, if you love your next-door neighbors, that's good. But if they and their yipping dog annoy you to no end, well, there's nothing you can do about it. You can't force yourself to love them.

In short, we think of love as a whimsical muse. If the muse strikes us, we're inspired. If not, we're indifferent.

But love in the Bible is a very different thing. For one, love can be commanded. The Bible commands us over and over again to love God (Deut. 6:4–6), our neighbor (Lev. 19:18), our fellow Christians (1 Pet. 4:8; John 13:34–35), and even our enemies (Rom. 12:19–21). Certainly love can grow cold (Matt. 24:12), and we can lose the love we had at first (Rev. 2:4). But Scripture commands us to love each other genuinely, affectionately, and earnestly (Rom. 12:9, 10; 1 Pet. 1:22), and to love God with all we've got (Deut. 6:4–6; Matt. 22:37–39). Love is not an arbitrary dictator summoning and dismissing us at whim, but something that can be commanded and striven for, something we can even stir up in others (Heb. 10:24).

Not only that, our love is fundamentally a response to

God's love: "We love because he first loved us" (1 John 4:19). God's love for us in Christ is what enables us to love others. It draws us and drives us to love others. And it shows us what love should look like.

In other words, our love is not like the wind. Nor is it something we rev ourselves up like a speedboat. Rather, our love is like a sailboat driven along by the wind of God's love. Our love, for God and everyone else, is always dependent on God's prior love for us. It's a response to his love.

That's one of the most important reasons why sound doctrine is for love.

SOUND DOCTRINE IS FOR LOVE

Many today view love and doctrine as enemies, or at best as rivals. Even in evangelical churches you'll hear echoes of Burt Bacharach and the Beatles: "What the world needs now is love, and love is all we need." Some say that doctrine only gets in the way. It puffs people up in pride. It inflates the head at the expense of the heart. Yet Scripture tells a different story.

Consider the neglected little gem of a letter we call 2 John. In fact, don't just consider it—go read it. All of it. If you're a slow reader, it will take you two minutes. It's right by the end of the Bible, just a few pages before Revelation. Go ahead. I'll wait right here.

Okay, back?

Did you notice all that the apostle John says about love and truth? He addresses his letter to "the elect lady and her children" (2 John 1:1), which is probably a way of referring to a local church (see the similar expression in v. 13). John loves this church "in truth," as do all who know the truth (v. 1). Why do John and his fellow believers love these other Christians? Answer: "Because of the truth that abides in us and will be with us forever" (v. 2).

So John and his fellow Christians love this church *in the truth* and *because of the truth*. Truth is the basis of our love for one another. It knits our hearts into one. John Stott, commenting on these verses, observes, "If we are Christians, we are to love our neighbours and even our enemies; but we are bound to our fellow Christians by the special bond of truth. Truth is the ground of reciprocal Christian love."[1]

John goes on to say that he rejoiced greatly to hear about those in the church who were walking in the truth (2 John 4). Then he asks his readers to keep the command they've had from the beginning, which is that they love one another (v. 5). This love consists in walking according to God's commandments, which is what we have heard from the beginning (v. 6).

Then, in verses 7 through 11, John reveals the pressing burden that prompted him to write: "Many deceivers have gone out into the world, those who do not confess the coming of Jesus Christ in the flesh" (v. 7). Therefore they should watch out for these false teachers (v. 8). To believe in a false gospel is to be cut off from God, but to remain in the truth is to remain with the Father and the Son (v. 9). They should not even extend hospitality to a false teacher because whoever does so "takes part in his wicked works" (vv. 10–11).

Why does John talk about walking in love in one breath

---

[1] John R. W. Stott, *The Letters of John: An Introduction and Commentary*, Tyndale New Testament Commentaries, 2nd ed. (Downers Grove, IL: InterVarsity Press, 1988), 205.

and false teaching in the next? Is he just jamming two unrelated topics together? Not at all. John wants these Christians to be united in a love that flows from the truth. Therefore they must not allow false teaching to enter their assembly and hack away at the roots of their love.

Second John teaches us that in the church, sound doctrine is the basis of our love for one another. It's the ground of our love. It leads us to love. It's the reason for our special bond as Christians. To put it the other way around, love is the goal of sound doctrine. If we don't love one another, then we haven't been properly gripped by the truth.

Sound doctrine is for love.

SOUND DOCTRINE IS FOR LOVE—ALL KINDS OF LOVE

Sound doctrine isn't merely the basis of our love for fellow Christians; it's the basis for *all* our love. Remember, sound doctrine is a summary of the Bible's teaching that is both faithful to the Bible and useful for life. Consider a few examples of how different doctrines teach us to love.

(1) *The doctrine of God leads us to love God.* The better we know him, the more we will love him. To know God better is to plumb more deeply the unfathomable depths of his love, and those depths call forth our love in response (Eph. 3:17–19).

(2) *The doctrine of man guides us to love our neighbors.* Because every human being is made in the image of God, every human being is worthy of our love (James 3:9). The doctrine of man teaches us to love others—all others. We should also show special love to those who are in need of provision and protection, because God does. He "executes justice for the fa-

therless and the widow, and loves the sojourner, giving him food and clothing" (Deut. 10:18).

(3) *The doctrine of providence teaches us to love our enemies.* Jesus observes that God causes the sun to rise on the evil and the good, and he sends rain on the righteous and the unrighteous (Matt. 5:43–48). The lesson for us? We, too, should love our enemies (vv. 44–45).

(4) *The doctrine of redemption teaches husbands to love their wives.* Paul writes, "Husbands, love your wives as Christ loved the church and gave himself for her, that he might sanctify her by the washing of water with the word" (Eph. 5:25–26). The love of Christ displayed in the gospel provides the pattern—and the motive—for a husband's love for his wife.

(5) *The doctrine of God's love trains all of God's people to love our fellow believers.* John writes, "In this is love, not that we have loved God but that he loved us and sent his Son to be the propitiation for our sins. Beloved, if God so loved us, we also ought to love one another" (1 John 4:10–11; see also John 13:34–35). Paul also tells all of us to "walk in love" toward each other, "as Christ loved us and gave himself up for us, a fragrant offering and sacrifice to God" (Eph. 5:2). The more we learn about how God has loved us in Christ, the better we'll know how to love one another and the more eager we'll be to love one another.

Sound doctrine holds before our eyes the length and breadth and height and depth of God's love (Eph. 3:18). It calls us to marvel at it, to praise God for it, and to be changed by it. By the power of the Spirit, when we meditate on the love God has demonstrated toward us in Christ (Rom. 5:8), our hearts are filled with love—for God, our neighbors, and our brothers and sisters in Christ. Here's how eighteenth-century pastor Jonathan Edwards put it:

> The work of redemption which the gospel makes known, above all things affords motives to love; for that work was the most glorious and wonderful exhibition of love that ever was seen or heard of. . . . True discoveries of the divine character dispose us to love God as the supreme good; they unite the heart in love to Christ; they incline the soul to flow out in love to God's people, and to all mankind.[2]

Sound doctrine also provides the pattern for our love. We are to walk in love *as* Christ has loved us. Husbands are to love their wives *as* Christ loved the church and gave himself for it. Just as Christ did not love us merely in "word or talk but in deed and in truth," so we also must love one another in tangible and costly ways (1 John 3:16–18).

Sound doctrine is for love—every kind of love.

DOCTRINE AND LOVE IN OUR LIVES AND CHURCHES

What difference should this make in our lives and our churches?

For one thing, it presents a solution for lovelessness. If your love for God is growing cold, you can turn up the heat by taking a big dose of sound doctrine, prayerfully meditating on it, and pressing it into your heart. Jonathan Edwards again: "When the truth of the glorious doctrines and promises of the

---

[2] Jonathan Edwards, *Charity and Its Fruits* (repr.; Edinburgh: Banner of Truth, 1969), 19, 21.

gospel is seen, these doctrines and promises are like so many cords which take hold of the heart, and draw it out in love to God and Christ."[3]

Or perhaps you're struggling to love another person. Maybe it's a difficult family member, an overbearing boss, or a church member who's giving you the cold shoulder. Stop and patiently consider how deeply you have been loved by God in Christ. "For one will scarcely die for a righteous person . . . but God shows his love for us in that while we were still sinners, Christ died for us" (Rom. 5:7–8). Christian, this is how God has loved you. When you were his enemy, he reconciled you to himself by the death of his Son (Rom. 5:9). The road to greater love for others begins with a deepening appreciation of the length and breadth and height and depth of God's love for you, which shines most brilliantly in the gospel of his Son.

And, as we've already seen, the love God has shown us in Christ is the basis of our love for one another in the church. Do you love other Christians only because of what you can get from them, or because both you and they are loved by God? Do you love fellow believers even when they provide plenty of reasons not to love them? Does your love extend to fellow church members across differences that, in the world, typically shut out love, like differences of wealth, social status, or skin color?

In fact, the Bible makes our love for our brothers and sisters in Christ the test of whether we really do know the love of Christ. "If anyone says, 'I love God,' and hates his brother, he is

---

[3] Ibid., 21.

a liar; for he who does not love his brother whom he has seen cannot love God whom he has not seen" (1 John 4:20; see also 1 John 3:17–18).

Our churches should be characterized by a mutual love that extends to all those who call upon the name of the Lord Jesus Christ, and love, don't forget, is fueled by sound doctrine. If bitterness, gossip, and slander are tearing your church apart, sound doctrine is one of the most necessary tools for sewing it back together. If rivalries and divisions are suffocating the church's love, it needs to breathe anew the rich air of sound doctrine. In order to love the unlovely and to reconcile enemies, we must remember that God has done those very things for us in Christ.

If there are people in our churches who are hard to love, well, so are we. That didn't stop our Savior from loving us all the way to the cross. The more deeply we are shaped by that truth, the more our lives and our churches will be conformed to the image of his love.

LIKE A SAIL THAT CATCHES THE WIND

Unlike a wind that dies and leaves you stranded at sea, God's love is a steady gale that never lets up. Not even our sin can threaten his love for us. In fact, the greatness of his love is shown precisely in that he loves us despite our sin.

God's love is an expression of his nature. "But God, being rich in mercy, because of the great love with which he loved us, even when we were dead in our trespasses, made us alive together with Christ" (Eph. 2:4–5). God is rich in mercy—he's got the stuff in spades. God revealed himself to Moses as "The

LORD, the LORD, a God merciful and gracious, slow to anger, and abounding in steadfast love and faithfulness, keeping steadfast love for thousands, forgiving iniquity and transgression and sin" (Ex. 34:6–7). And John captures it all in just a few words: "Anyone who does not love does not know God, because God is love" (1 John 4:8).

God is love, and he has loved us wondrously in Christ. His love for us is the basis, source, and pattern of our love for him, our neighbors, our fellow Christians, and even our enemies. Our love answers his, like a sail that catches the wind.

Sound doctrine is for love.

5

SOUND DOCTRINE IS FOR UNITY

Jason is one of my best friends from college. We met through a campus ministry during our freshman year, joined the same church, and wound up rooming together. During those years a friendship was forged that continues to bring mutual encouragement, sharpening, and joy.

Jason and I are both from California. We're both white males. We're both musicians—Jason is a very gifted classical pianist. We're both bookish, though also talkative. You might say we have a lot in common.

On the other hand, we come from different family backgrounds. Different economic circumstances, too. And we've got pretty different personalities, which is where the real fun begins.

For his part, Jason is certain that he never would have been my friend if we were not both Christians. Maybe it's because I'm cool and he's a nerd? (Not true.) Maybe it's our different backgrounds. (That may be part of it.) Maybe it's that my personality so vexes Jason that he never would have put up with me apart from the indwelling of the Holy Spirit. (Now we're getting warmer.)

Whatever the reason, Jason is utterly convinced that he never would have been my friend apart from Christ. Over the years he has told me this often and in no uncertain terms. It almost makes me feel a little insecure! Am I really that hard to like? That overbearing? That obnoxiously self-assured?

But my point is, despite our differences, Jason and I are great friends. And, at least according to Jason, that never would have happened apart from the gospel.

HOW CAN THE CHURCH BRING TOGETHER WHAT THE WORLD TEARS APART?

The gospel-enabled friendship that Jason and I enjoy is a mere glimmer of the glorious display of unity that is the church of the Lord Jesus Christ.

In order to find unity, Jason and I did have to work through some barriers—mainly the barrier of my troublesome personality. But the world is torn by divisions that run much deeper than that. Issues of ethnicity, social status, and gender come quickly to mind.

Our society prides itself on tolerance and inclusion, yet dozens of deep-seated divisions seal off entire categories of people from each other. Worse, such divisions turn people against each other, despite many good efforts to the contrary. For instance, in America today, racial discrimination is not only legislated against but stigmatized, yet racism still runs deep in our hearts and minds. And it doesn't take much to bring it to the surface.

Yet the church really does transcend these differences and divisions: "There is neither Jew nor Greek, there is neither slave nor free, there is neither male nor female, for you are all one in Christ Jesus" (Gal. 3:28; see also Col. 3:11).

How can Paul say this? How can the church transcend these divisions that continue to defy the world's best efforts to overcome them?

In Galatians, Paul treats the unity of Jew and Greek, slave and free, male and female as an inference from the fact that we are justified—declared righteous by God—on the basis of faith alone, not on the basis of any good works that we do. The Galatians were beginning to rely on circumcision and observance of the law for salvation (Gal. 3:1; 5:2–4). So Paul reminds them that we are declared righteous in God's sight "by faith in Christ and not by works of the law" (Gal. 2:16).

Therefore, the ethnic Jews or law-abiding converts to Judaism among them could claim no superiority over their Gentile brothers: "Know then that it is those of faith who are the sons of Abraham" (Gal. 3:7). Right standing before God, and therefore membership in God's people, are given by God's grace alone through faith alone in Christ alone. Therefore, right standing before God and membership in God's people are available to *all* who come to Christ in faith, regardless of ethnicity, social status, gender, or anything else.

In other words, the doctrine of justification by faith alone is the foundation of the church's unity. All those who have come to Christ and confessed their faith through baptism have "put on Christ" (Gal. 3:27) and are heirs of all the promises of God (Gal. 3:29). And since we in the church have all "put on Christ," we are all one in Christ (Gal. 3:28).

Christ alone is the doorway into the church. You don't have to be able to trace your genealogy back to Abraham. You don't have to belong to a certain political party or live in a certain part of town. You don't have to hold a certain degree or make a certain amount of money. All are invited to put faith in Christ, and so all who do are welcomed into the church as brothers and sisters, family members on equal footing in the household of God.

The unity of the church is founded on, and flows from, the doctrine of justification by faith alone. That's one of many ways in which sound doctrine is for unity.

SOUND DOCTRINE IS FOR UNITY

A similar lesson can be found in 1 Corinthians. Paul was prompted to write to the Corinthians because of their quarreling and one-upmanship: "Each one of you says, 'I follow Paul,' or 'I follow Apollos,' or 'I follow Cephas,' or 'I follow Christ'" (1 Cor. 1:12). Paul's response to this division is striking: "Is Christ divided? Was Paul crucified for you? Or were you baptized in the name of Paul?" (1 Cor. 1:13).

Paul is saying that the church should be no more divided than Christ. Why? Because the church is the body of Christ, as Paul explains at length in chapter 12. Further, people should not put their ultimate allegiance in anyone besides Christ, since it was Christ who was crucified for our sins (see 1 Cor. 15:1–4). And Christians are baptized into the name of the triune God, not any human teacher (see Matt. 28:19). So Christians belong to the Lord, not to any teacher.

All of these rhetorical questions in 1 Corinthians 1:13 mount theological arguments for the church's unity. Since we are the body of Christ, we should be united, not divided. Since our ultimate allegiance is to him, and we are baptized into his name, we must not divide our churches into factions around our favorite leaders.

The unity of the church is founded on and flows from sound doctrine. Again, sound doctrine is a summary of the Bible's teaching that is both faithful to the Bible and useful for life. So when the unity of the Corinthian church is imperiled, Paul drills down to theological foundations to bring them back into conformity with God's plan. Sound doctrine is not only the foundation of unity, it's the restorer of unity. It not only provides the pattern for unity, it helps to realign a church with that pattern when it has been bent out of shape. Sound doctrine is for unity.

We see this same dynamic in Ephesians 4, where Paul urges us to walk in a manner worthy of our calling (v. 1). How should we do this? By being humble, gentle, and patient, bearing with each other in love, and being "eager to maintain the unity of the Spirit in the bond of peace" (vv. 2–3). Our main callings as Christians include loving one another, bearing humbly with one another, and working hard to preserve the unity of the church.

Why should we do this? Paul answers by taking us to the deepest realities of our faith: "There is one body and one Spirit—just as you were called to the one hope that belongs to your call—one Lord, one faith, one baptism, one God and Father of all, who is over all and through all and in all" (Eph. 4:4–6). Everything about our faith proclaims, "Unity!" There is one body of Christ. There is one Spirit who gives us new life. There is one hope to which we were called. There is one Lord Jesus Christ, one faith in that same Lord, and one baptism into his name. There is one Father over all. And Father, Son, and Spirit are one God.

The unity of the church is grounded in the unity of the faith. Therefore, we are called to preserve the bond of peace which ties us together, the unity which the Spirit has given us. Because the church really is one, we are called to be one.

NEEDLE AND THREAD TO REPAIR THE FABRIC OF UNITY

Sadly, too often our churches are not unified. Too often we are fragmented along the same lines that divide non-Christians from each other. Too often we allow bitterness, envy, gossip, pride, rivalries, and judgmentalism to seize the fragile fabric of unity and rip it to shreds.

It's not surprising, then, that Scripture exhorts us to pursue, maintain, and repair unity within our churches. Paul writes to the Philippians, "So if there is any encouragement in Christ, any comfort from love, any participation in the Spirit, any affection and sympathy, complete my joy by being of the same mind, having the same love, being in full accord and of one mind" (Phil. 2:1–2). As in 1 Corinthians 1 and Ephesians 4, Paul appeals to the doctrinal roots of our unity. He appeals to the blessings of the gospel in order to say essentially, "If you've tasted the goodness of the gospel's blessings, then please, please preserve this one—the unity of the church."

Notice that he's aiming for comprehensive unity—unity of mind and heart, of thought and affection. He wants the church to be as tightly knit together as the cotton threads in our clothes that blend into one seamless fabric. He wants the church's unity to be as pure and resonant as an orchestra tuned to the same pitch.

How should a church pursue this unity? "Do nothing from selfish ambition or conceit, but in humility count others more significant than yourselves. Let each of you look not only to his own interests, but also to the interests of others" (Phil. 2:3–4). Humility serves unity. When we consider others more important than ourselves, we set our agendas aside and serve them. We relax our grip on what we want, and reach out to others instead.

Then Paul reiterates his charge: "Have this mind among yourselves, which is yours in Christ Jesus" (Phil. 2:5). What mind is that? The mind that led Christ not to count equality with God a thing to be grasped, but to become a servant; the mind that was willing to be obedient to the point of death on a cross. That's the mind which Paul exhorts us to have (Phil. 2:6–9).

Paul exhorts the Philippians to humility in the service of unity, in imitation of the Lord who humbled himself in order to save us. This passage, in other words, fuses together doctrine and exhortation as tightly as possible. We have received the mind of Christ, as well as encouragement in him and fellowship with the Spirit (Phil. 2:1–2, 5), all because of his self-abasing sacrifice for us (Phil. 2:6–11). In his incarnation, humiliation, and crucifixion, Jesus considered us more important than himself. He didn't look to his own interests, but to ours. He didn't seek his own good, but the good of others.

These rich doctrinal teachings, then, form the pattern that we should trace out in the life of the church. These weighty reflections on the work of Christ show us the footsteps we must walk in. Jesus is our Savior and our example. We grow in humility, a key ingredient for unity, when we consider what Jesus has done for us, and how he now calls us to follow in the same path.

Rivalry and conceit are about as practical as problems in a church get, yet Scripture's solution to them is not merely practical, but doctrinal. The incarnation of Christ teaches us humility. Christ's humiliation and substitutionary death teach us to put the interests of our fellow church members before our own. Because Jesus served not himself but us, we are called to serve others.

Sound doctrine is the ground and source of the church's unity. It's the pattern for the church's unity. Not only that, it equips us to pursue and preserve and repair the church's unity. It inoculates us against divisiveness. It smothers the fires of rivalry. And it helps to stitch together the garment of the church's unity that we too easily tear apart.

PURSUE A STRONGER AND MORE FLEXIBLE UNITY

Like a fine silk dress, the unity of the church is both precious and delicate. As the psalmist puts it: "Behold, how good and pleasant it is when brothers dwell in unity! . . . It is like the dew of Hermon, which falls on the mountains of Zion! For there the Lord has commanded the blessing, life forevermore" (Ps. 133:1, 3). Yet how easy it is for bitterness to supplant sweetness, discord to displace harmony, and factions to replace friendship.

That's why we must not unify our churches around anything but the gospel and the doctrines that flow from and undergird the gospel. It's all too easy to unite our churches around things besides sound doctrine, like political stances, schooling methods, music style, organic food, denominational traditions, or just about anything else.

In most churches, members will have much in common besides their faith, but the faith of the Scriptures is what our unity should consist in. It should be the substance, the ground, and the basis of our unity.

The test of this is whether we can love fellow members who confess the same faith yet who differ with us over politics, schooling options, the foods we eat, or music preferences. Can we put their interests before our own? Can we embrace our brothers and sisters who are united with us in sound doctrine but who are culturally or ethnically different from us, or who have different opinions about any number of issues? If not, then our unity isn't founded on the gospel and sound doctrine, but on human preferences and traditions.

Church unity is often fragile because it's built from the wrong stuff. Unity around cultural customs and personal preferences is brittle: put a little pressure on it and it will shatter. But unity around sound doctrine is strong and flexible, like a sturdy wood-frame house built on a good foundation. When storms blow against it, it may sway and groan a little in the wind, but it will hold together.

Sound doctrine is the substance and center of our unity in the church. So we should unify our churches around true biblical doctrine, not cultural customs, politics, or anything else.

A UNITY THAT DEFIES EXPLANATION

Through the gospel—and only through the gospel—our churches can display a unity that baffles the world. That unity, therefore, witnesses to the power of the gospel. Jesus prayed that his people would be one so that the world would come to believe that he is from God (John 17:20–21). The unity of the church displays God's wisdom to all creation, including heavenly powers (Eph. 3:10).

The doctrinally driven unity of the church defies human explanations. Only God can knit into one body Jew and Gentile, slave and free, Democrat and Republican, homeschooler and public-schooler. And he does this through the gospel, by which everyone who trusts in Christ is counted righteous and welcomed into his people.

So pray for your church's unity. Pursue it. Preserve it. Repair it when it tears. Do this by turning again and again to the great doctrines of Scripture, because sound doctrine is for unity.

6

SOUND DOCTRINE
IS FOR WORSHIP

Do you ever get "story grip"? It's the condition caused by read-ing a book that is so compelling that the book won't let you put it down.

You stay up way too late ("I'm just going to finish this chapter. And the next one."). You neglect important tasks ("The trash can wait.") and people ("Sorry, honey, were you saying something?"). Wittingly or unwittingly, you seal your-self off from the rest of the world until you finish the book.

When it's over, you walk around in a daze, still half stuck in the book. The characters who were your companions for a few days now haunt your thoughts like ghosts as you return to real life.

The last time I got story grip, I had been reading a long-ish novel when I should have been studying for an intensive summer theology class. So one night I had to escape from the book's clutches and stay up late reading a dense, dry textbook about modern theologians. I kept dozing off about three times per page, and every time I did, something strange happened. As I started to drift into sleep, the words of the theology textbook would morph into the characters and events in the novel I had been reading. My brain was so absorbed in the story that it pushed its way to the surface of my mind and spilled onto the pages before me.

Clearly, story grip is not always desirable. There's a time and a place for an addictive book, and there are many more times and places for keeping such a book safely on the shelf.

But, especially for a nerd like me, there's something deeply satisfying about getting lost in the pages of a book. You're totally focused, yet completely relaxed. You're perfectly calm, yet the thrill of the story can make your heart race.

Of course, books aren't the only things that can grip us. Have you ever been on a hike through the mountains when, turning a corner, the view struck you dumb? Have you ever been so wrapped up in a conversation with a friend that the first time you stopped to look at the clock it was already 2:00 a.m.? Have you ever put a song on repeat for hours on end, somehow finding that you liked it even more the fifty-third time than you did the first?

There are some things we not only enjoy but delight in. Things that carry us out of ourselves. Things we get lost in, and love it.

SOUND DOCTRINE IS FOR WORSHIP

Many Christians look for this kind of experience in worship, specifically the church's times of corporate worship. And that's not all wrong. Worshiping God should grip our minds and hearts. It should carry us out of ourselves.

But the problem is that, especially when it comes to corporate worship, we can fall into the trap of thinking that the purpose of worship is to have an intense emotional experience. We can view worship mainly as a time for us to express ourselves, to get lost in the moment. We even begin thinking that worship, frankly, is about us.

But of course we know that worship is not about us—it's about God. Psalm 29:2 tells us, "Ascribe to the LORD the glory due his name." Worship, as the Bible defines it, is giving to God the glory that he deserves because of who he is and what he has done for us in Christ. Worship is about giving God the heartfelt adoration, praise, and obedience that he is due. Which is why sound doctrine is for worship.

SOUND DOCTRINE IS FUEL FOR WORSHIP

Sound doctrine is for worship like wood is for a fire. If you want a roaring blaze that lasts through the evening, you pile on crisp, dry logs. So sound doctrine fuels our worship.

D. A. Carson has said, "What ought to make worship delightful to us is not, in the first instance, its novelty or its aesthetic beauty, but its object: God himself is delightfully wonderful, and we learn to delight in him."[1] Sound doctrine teaches us to delight in God because it shows us how delightful God is. It holds before our eyes the perfections of his character, the abundance of his grace, and the majesty of his sovereign rule over all things.

Sound doctrine tells us why we should worship God. And

---

[1] D. A. Carson, "Worship under the Word," in *Worship by the Book*, ed. D. A. Carson (Grand Rapids: Zondervan, 2002), 30.

sound doctrine, when thoroughly kneaded into our hearts, draws out and motivates our worship.

We see this all over the place in the Psalms. For instance, take Psalm 95. It begins with a stirring summons to worship: "Oh come, let us sing to the LORD; let us make a joyful noise to the rock of our salvation! Let us come into his presence with thanksgiving; let us make a joyful noise to him with songs of praise!" (vv. 1–2).

But the psalm doesn't simply command us to worship; it also tells us why: "For the LORD is a great God, and a great King above all gods. In his hand are the depths of the earth; the heights of the mountains are his also. The sea is his, for he made it, and his hands formed the dry land" (vv. 3–5). Do you see that little word "for" at the beginning of verse 3? The psalm is giving us reasons to worship God. It's grounding our praise in God's inherent worthiness to be worshiped. We should worship God, verse 3 says, because he is great. He is exalted as King above all so-called "gods." We should worship God because he alone is the sovereign King over all the earth. God has no rival in heaven, and he should have no rival in our hearts.

Verses 4 and 5 give us further proof of God's greatness. They remind us that God created the world, and therefore God owns the world. The highest mountain peaks and the deepest reaches of the seas are all his. God alone created and upholds and rules over the earth.

Therefore we, as God's creatures, are bound to pour out our hearts to him in grateful, adoring, awestruck praise. We should sing to him for the same reason the angels sang when God created the heavens and the earth: because all of creation displays the glory, power, wisdom, beauty, and awesome rule of God.

After this, the psalm again calls us to worship: "Oh come, let us worship and bow down; let us kneel before the LORD, our Maker!" (v. 6). Again the Psalm gives us reasons to worship: "For he is our God, and we are the people of his pasture, and the sheep of his hand" (v. 7a). God is *our* God. He has bound himself to us, to do good to us (Jer. 32:40). And he has made us his own. We are his people, and he is our Shepherd (Pss. 23:1–6; 100:3). He cares for us personally; he feeds us from his own hand. Those same omnipotent hands that hold granite peaks in their grip care for us, provide for us, and gently lead us in the way we should go. The majestic, exalted ruler of all has stooped low and come down to us.

Scripture teaches us that God has rescued us from our sin, reconciled us to himself, and pledged himself to provide for all of our needs, now and forever. All of these are reasons to praise him, to adore him, to make a joyful noise to him, and to bow down before him in submission and obedience. All of this is what the Bible means by "worship." And such worship, Psalm 95 shows, is fueled by sound doctrine.

SOUND DOCTRINE TEACHES US HOW TO WORSHIP

Yet sound doctrine is for worship not only like fuel for a fire; it's also like a script for a play. In his Word, God teaches us how we should worship him. Sound doctrine—specifically, right teaching about how we are to worship God—enables worship that is pleasing to God.

Throughout Scripture, God again and again shows us that

he cares about how we worship him. When God called Israel to himself and gave them his law, he told them not to worship other gods, and he also told them not to worship *him* through images (Ex. 20:2–6; Deut 4:15–18; 12:31). As Ligon Duncan puts it, "This reminds us that there are two ways to commit idolatry: worship something other than the true God or worship the true God the wrong way."[2] Further, God commanded the Israelites to be careful not to add to or take away from anything he commanded concerning how they were to worship him (Deut. 12:29–32). Even seemingly slight deviations from God's revealed plans for their worship carried serious consequences (1 Sam. 15:22; 2 Sam. 6:5–7). From the beginning, God has been concerned with the "how" of worship.

But that was Israel under the old covenant. What about the church under the new covenant? As Christians, the form and substance of our worship certainly differ from how Israel was commanded to worship God, yet God is no less concerned about how we worship him. True, the New Testament doesn't lay out a model order of service that every church should follow. But it does tell us, whether by command or example, what to do in our corporate assemblies. We should read and preach the Bible (1 Tim. 4:13; 2 Tim. 4:2); pray (1 Tim. 2:8); sing psalms, hymns, and spiritual songs (Eph. 5:18–19; Col. 3:16–17); and celebrate the Lord's Supper and baptism (Matt. 28:19; 1 Cor. 11:23–26).

The New Testament also talks about *how* we should wor-

---

[2] J. Ligon Duncan III, "Does God Care How We Worship?" in *Give Praise to God: A Vision for Reforming Worship*, eds. Philip Graham Ryken, Derek W. H. Thomas, and J. Ligon Duncan III (Phillipsburg, NJ: P&R, 2003), 33. Much of what I'm saying in this paragraph is drawn from this excellent chapter.

ship. We are to worship God thankfully (Col. 3:17), reverently (Heb. 12:28–29), in unity (Rom. 15:6), in Spirit and truth (John 4:24), in an orderly fashion (1 Cor. 14:40), and in a manner calculated to build up the whole body (1 Cor. 14:12, 26).

All of our corporate worship, in fact, has a horizontal dimension as well. When we sing, for example, we address not only God but one another (Eph. 5:18–19; Col. 3:16–17). Corporate worship is not about having your personal devotions with a hundred other people in the room. Instead, it's about building up the body of Christ even as we give praise to God.

Of course, worship is not limited to what we do in church. Paul says that our whole lives should be offered as sacrifices of worship to God (Rom. 12:1–2). But whether we're talking about corporate worship or "all of life" worship, Scripture has a lot to say about the what, the why, and the how.

In order to worship God rightly, we need to know how God wants to be worshiped, and he has revealed this to us in his Word. Therefore, sound doctrine teaches us how to worship. It trains us to follow the script for worship that God himself has written.

SOUND DOCTRINE SHAPES, FEEDS, INFORMS, AND MOTIVATES OUR WORSHIP

What does this mean for our lives and churches?

First, if sound doctrine is for worship, then sound doctrine should shape the substance and even the style of our worship. God has told us how we are to worship him, so we should do what he says. And the "how" of worship should always be filtered through the character of God. Certainly a wide range of styles and cultural expressions can bring God glory. But the first question we should always ask about, say, a particular worship song, is not whether we like the style, but whether it honors God. And that is chiefly, though not exclusively, a matter of verbal content.

Second, because sound doctrine is what fuels worship, our corporate worship services (and private devotional lives) should constantly feed on it. Christians are moved to worship when we are awed by the greatness and glory of God, and the wonder of the salvation he has accomplished for us. Churches should therefore sing Scripture-soaked, doctrine-rich songs and hymns. We should read the Bible corporately, as Scripture commands (1 Tim. 4:13), which is itself an act of worship. And our prayers, like biblical prayers, should be packed with meditations on who God is and what he's done for us in Christ. In short, our worship should be filled to the brim with sound doctrine.

Third, sound doctrine should inform and explain worship. Why do we pray and sing to God? Why do we listen to God's Word? Why do we celebrate the Lord's Supper? Sound doctrine reminds us why we worship God, and it illumines our acts of worship. Without the crisp light of sound doctrine shining on it, worship can become shadowy and unintelligible. In worship our minds and spirits must be equally engaged (1 Cor. 14:15). Therefore, those who lead our services should explain why we do what we do. Sound doctrine should form the background that enables each worshiper to engage with a united heart and an understanding mind.

Fourth, sound doctrine should motivate worship. Like

love—which is an essential component of worship—worship is a response to God, to who he is and what he's done for us. Therefore, church leaders should motivate their people to worship by proclaiming sound doctrine. If you want your people to praise God, show them the greatness of God. If you want them to bring God glory, show them God's glory. If you want them to fall before God in loving submission, then exult in his sovereign rule in your preaching and teaching.

Worship is neither an emotional ecstasy to be whipped up, nor a zen state of mind to be gained through relaxation. Instead, it's the response of our heart, mind, soul, and strength to God, to his glorious being and his mighty acts. So we stir up worship not by focusing on worship, but by filling the mind's eye with a panoramic vision of the beauty and holiness of God.

This means that music is not what drives our worship. Instead, music—by which I mean congregational singing—is a vehicle for our worship. If your heart and mind are not responding to the inexpressible majesty of God, you're not worshiping, no matter how passionately you may be enjoying a musical experience.

What's more, worship is even less dependent on the instrumentation that accompanies our singing. Instrumental music in church should *support* congregational singing, but a certain style of music is not the key that unlocks our worship. That key is the glory and majesty of God.

Sound doctrine should drive the substance and style of our worship. It should fill the content of our worship. And it should motivate our worship, since worship is always a response to the glory and grace of God.

HOW TO LOSE YOURSELF IN WORSHIP

We should lose ourselves in worship, but not in the way that we sometimes think.

You don't get gripped by a story from fixating on whether or not you're having a fulfilling reading experience. Instead, you're gripped when the story is so compelling that you forget all about yourself and how long you've been reading.

You don't get struck dumb by a mountaintop view if you're staring at your shoes. The shoes might have brought you there, but the view is what you're there for.

You don't lose yourself in worship by trying to lose yourself in worship. Instead, aim to glorify God as he deserves and desires. Necessary equipment for this is a mind and heart that are filled with the truth about him. Each time you absorb more sound doctrine, you stoke the fires of worship.

The Bible's revelation of God's character and saving work provides fuel for worship and a script for worship. It shapes, feeds, informs, drives, and motivates our worship.

Sound doctrine is for worship.

7

SOUND DOCTRINE
IS FOR WITNESS

A former music teacher of mine had a sign on his office door that read, "Practide madrw pwrfeft." Below that it read, "Practice madrw pwrfeft." The sign kept cleaning up its act letter by letter until at the bottom it finally stated, "Practice makes perfect."

"Practice makes perfect" is a well-worn cliché, but it's well-worn because it wears well. Practice can be repetitive, dull, and tedious, but it's essential to improvement. Practice requires discipline, willpower, and sheer effort, but the payoff can be enormous—and we aren't likely to improve any other way.

When I was a full-time musician, I would sometimes practice for three or four hours in an afternoon before playing a concert all evening. On some of those nights, my saxophone would begin to feel like an extension of myself. Through those long hours of practice, my mind began to connect with the instrument as if it were part of my body. By living in the world of notes in the day, I could speak their language more fluently onstage at night.

For a jazz musician, practice is essential on a number of fronts. It helps you to master the technical demands of your instrument. It enables you to memorize the songs and chord progressions that are the structures on which you improvise. And it builds up a vocabulary that you draw on to say new things, just like verbal vocabulary. Practicing jazz vocabulary gives you raw materials that you reshape and combine into something new every time you perform. So the more you practice, the more fluently you'll perform.

EVANGELISM PRACTICE WITH MARTIN LUTHER

During my sophomore year of college, I had a strikingly similar experience with evangelism.

For a couple years I had been joining several fellow Christian students to share the gospel on our sunny Southern California campus. On one occasion, I had spent a couple hours before our meeting time reading Martin Luther's classic *The Bondage of the Will*. It's a witty and rigorous exposition of Scripture's teaching that, apart from Christ, our wills are enslaved to sin, and only the sovereign grace of God can free us.

So I met up with my friends and we divided into twos to walk around and start conversations. Before long, I struck up a conversation with a friendly philosophy student. After I shared the gospel with him, the first words out of his mouth were, "What about free will?"

I thought to myself, "Funny you should ask!" Then I explained to him that the Bible holds people responsible for our actions—we're willing and accountable moral agents. Yet our wills are totally given over to sin. We're enslaved to it. Left to ourselves, people always choose evil and reject God. We need God to save us.

My two hours of reading theology that afternoon turned out to be evangelism practice. I didn't know it at the time, but it was about to come in handy in an extremely practical way.

Sharing the gospel that day felt like performing at night after a long afternoon of practice. The words came more naturally. I was more comfortable than usual thinking on my feet. I was more confident in answering this individual's questions from Scripture.

On that afternoon, sound doctrine directly informed, enabled, and equipped my witness to the gospel. It enabled me to present biblical truth to a skeptic. It put Bible verses and biblical arguments right at my fingertips that otherwise might have been out of reach.

Like practice is for performance, sound doctrine is for witness.

SOUND DOCTRINE IS FOR WITNESS

By "witness" I'm primarily referring to evangelism. Evangelism is sharing the good news about Jesus with those who don't believe in him, and it's calling them to turn from their sin and trust in him. What is that good news? Here it is in four parts:

- *God:* The one and only God, who is holy (Isa. 6:1–7), made us in his image to know and glorify him (Gen. 1:26–28).
- *Man:* But we sinned and cut ourselves off from him, so that God's wrath is now against us because of our sin (Genesis 3; Rom. 1:18; 3:23).

- *Christ:* In his great love, God sent his Son Jesus to come as king and rescue his people from their enemies—most significantly their own sin (Psalm 2; Luke 1:67–79). Jesus established his kingdom by acting as both a mediating priest and a priestly sacrifice: he lived a perfect life and died on the cross, thus fulfilling God's law himself and taking on himself the punishment for the sins of many (Mark 10:45; John 1:14; Rom. 3:21–26; 5:12–21; Heb. 7:26). Then, he rose again from the dead, showing that God accepted his sacrifice and that God's wrath against us had been exhausted (Acts 2:24; Rom. 4:25).
- *Response:* God now calls everyone to repent of their sins and trust in Christ alone for forgiveness (John 1:12; Acts 17:30). If we repent of our sins and trust in Christ, we are born again into a new, eternal life with God (John 3:16).

The gospel is this message of salvation through Christ, and evangelism, or "witnessing," is telling others this message and urging them to believe it.

Why then do I say that sound doctrine is for witness? First, the gospel *is* doctrine. And doctrine, remember, is putting the Bible into our own words. As Christians, we want to know how to bring into everyday conversation the biblical truth about who God is, who we are, what Jesus has done to save us, and what he calls us to do in response. If we do away with doctrine, we do away with the gospel and evangelism. Sound doctrine—gospel doctrine—is the content of our witness.

SOUND DOCTRINE: THE STORY AND WORLDVIEW THAT FRAME THE GOSPEL

Sound doctrine is also important for evangelism because it enables us to explain the gospel more fully. How? Sound doctrine teaches us the story that the gospel fulfills and completes, and the worldview within which the gospel makes sense.

Think about the importance of understanding the whole biblical story that the gospel completes—the narrative of creation and the fall, the exodus, Israel's conquest of the land, the judges and kings, and Israel's exile from their land and promised restoration. The better we know this story, the better we will understand the gospel, which is the fulfillment of this story. This is especially important for evangelizing people who have some knowledge of Scripture, such as those who have a Christian background, but have not repented of sin and trusted in Christ. When someone has a basic understanding of the Bible's storyline, we can build on that understanding and demonstrate how all the stories of Scripture find their ultimate meaning in the gospel.

The apostle Paul did just this in his own evangelism, especially with Jews. He set the good news about Jesus in the context of the whole story of the Bible. Speaking in one Jewish synagogue, Paul told of how God brought Israel out of Egypt, gave them the land of Canaan, set judges and kings over them, and promised that the son of one of these kings, David, would reign forever (Acts 13:17–22). Then he declared, "Of this man's offspring God has brought to Israel a Savior, Jesus, as he promised" (Acts 13:23). Next Paul explained how the life, death, and resurrection of Jesus fulfill all that God promised in the Old Testament (vv. 26–37). Then he concluded, "Let it be known to you therefore, brothers, that through this man forgiveness of sins is proclaimed to you, and by him everyone who believes is freed from everything from which you could not be freed by the law of Moses" (vv. 38–39). And he warned them not to reject this message (vv. 40–41).

For us today, too, it is important to understand the story of Scripture first of all in order to understand the gospel, and also to explain it to others.

Sound doctrine also provides not just the story but also the worldview that frames the gospel. We see this in another evangelistic speech by Paul. This time, Paul was addressing the Areopagus, the intellectual council of Athens, who were a group of polytheistic Greek philosophers (Acts 17:22–34). And here Paul begins with God. The deities of the Greeks were unpredictable and needy. Not so the true God, said Paul. The true God is the Creator and Lord of all. He is perfect in himself and is not lacking anything. Therefore, he does not need us to supply his wants through sacrifices (vv. 22–25).

Next Paul turned to the origin and nature of humanity. The Greeks believed that they belonged to a distinct, superior race of men. But Paul exploded this view by establishing that all people are created by God and descend from one man. Further, God is not removed from humanity, but gives life, sustains life, and ordains the circumstances of our lives (Acts 17:26–28).

In view of all this, Paul continues, all people are obligated to serve God. We are God's offspring, and we should know better than to commit idolatry. God has long been patient with humanity, but he now calls all people everywhere to repent, because one day he will judge all people "by a man whom he has appointed; and of this he has given assurance to all by raising him from the dead" (Acts 17:31). At this point in

Paul's speech, some mocked, but some eventually believed (vv. 32–34).

Based on Luke's summary, it's not clear whether Paul actually explained the message of Jesus's death and resurrection, or whether he simply mentioned the resurrection and was immediately cut off. But for our purposes, it's worth noticing that the doctrines Paul preached to these Greeks provided the worldview within which the gospel makes sense. You won't seek a savior unless you know you need saving. You won't know you need saving until you come face-to-face with the God to whom you're accountable. So Paul backs all the way up to the beginning and explains who God is, who we are, and what our obligations are to God.

Acts 17 is a case study in the importance of sound doctrine for evangelism. Paul packs so many doctrinal truths into this speech that it's hard to count them all:

- The existence, lordship, and self-sufficiency of the one true God (vv. 24–28);
- God's creation of the whole universe (v. 24);
- God's special creation of man and the unity of the human race (v. 26);
- God's providential rule over all of history and every human life (vv. 26–28);
- Man's responsibility to rightly serve God (vv. 29–30);
- The need for people to repent in order to find mercy from God (v. 30);
- The resurrection of Jesus Christ (v. 31);
- God's final judgment of all people (v. 31); and
- The lordship of Jesus Christ (v. 31).

We learn from Paul's speech in Acts 17 that sound doctrine is for witness in that it provides the worldview which frames the gospel. Sound doctrine provides the necessary preamble to the message about what Jesus has done to save sinners.

The lesson for us is this: when you're evangelizing someone who lacks even a basic knowledge of Scripture, use sound doctrine to fill in the background for them. Use sound doctrine to provide the foundation and scaffolding for the gospel. Use it to show people why they need saving in the first place.

Sound doctrine gives us the story that finds its fulfillment in the gospel and the worldview that enables us to understand the gospel. Sound doctrine frames the gospel, helping us explain it and make sense of it. Sound doctrine is for witness.

SOUND DOCTRINE MOTIVATES, FREES, EMBOLDENS, RENEWS, AND STRENGTHENS OUR WITNESS

Sound doctrine also motivates our witness. How? The better we know the gospel, the more motivated we'll be to share it. The more deeply we know Christ's love for us, the more his love will compel us to talk about it with others (2 Cor. 5:14). Knowing sound doctrine also gives us confidence to witness. The better we know the gospel, the more readily we'll share it with others.

Sound doctrine also frees us from false guilt about evangelism. Scripture teaches that only God can change people's hearts and minds. Only God can give life to the dead (Eph. 2:1–10) and sight to the blind (2 Cor. 4:3–6). Our job is to preach the gospel, plead with people to repent, and pray for God to act. That's it. We can't make anyone believe the gospel.

Many people don't evangelize because they're intimidated by the thought of trying to convince someone to become a Christian, but sound doctrine lifts this burden of guilt. We can't make anyone anything. All we can do—and must do—is preach the gospel and pray for God to save people.

And sound doctrine emboldens our witness. Some people think the doctrine of election—that God, out of sheer grace, has chosen those who will be saved—is a disincentive to evangelism, but we see the exact opposite in Scripture. For example, immediately after scaling the highest heights of this doctrine in Romans 9, in Romans 10 Paul issues a bold call for evangelism: "How then will they call on him in whom they have not believed? And how are they to believe in him of whom they have never heard? And how are they to hear without someone preaching?" (Rom. 10:14). Similarly, we read in Acts 18 of how the Lord encouraged Paul in his evangelism by saying, "Do not be afraid, but go on speaking and do not be silent, for I am with you, and no one will attack you to harm you, for I have many in this city who are my people" (Acts 18:9–10). Hearing that God had chosen many for salvation in the city of Corinth enabled Paul to preach boldly and without fear. The doctrine of election emboldens our witness.

Finally, sound doctrine, and the doctrine of election in particular, renews our commitment and strengthens our resolve in the face of failure or persecution. Contemplating his own imprisonment, Paul says, "But the word of God is not bound! Therefore I endure everything for the sake of the elect, that they also may obtain the salvation that is in Christ Jesus with eternal glory" (2 Tim. 2:9–10). If Paul endured through trials like imprisonment for the sake of those whom God has chosen, and continued to faithfully preach the gospel, so should we. The doctrine of election fueled Paul's perseverance in evangelism, and it should do the same for us. Sound doctrine is for witness.

THE FRUITS OF SOUND DOCTRINE ADORN AND STRENGTHEN OUR CHURCHES' WITNESS

This whole book is about how sound doctrine gives birth to godly lives and healthy churches. It's about the fruits that sound doctrine bears in the church, including holiness, love, unity, and worship. All of these fruits contribute to our gospel witness, as individuals and especially as local churches. These fruits of sound doctrine adorn our witness like a frame adorns a picture or jewelry adorns a woman (Titus 2:10).

Holiness: Peter exhorts us to be holy, keeping our conduct honorable among non-Christians, so that they may see our good deeds and "glorify God on the day of visitation" (1 Pet. 2:11–12; see also Matt. 5:13–16). Our holiness testifies to the power of the gospel and brings people to glorify God.

Love: Jesus commands, "Just as I have loved you, you also are to love one another. By this all people will know that you are my disciples, if you have love for one another" (John 13:34–35). Our love for our fellow church members displays the love of Christ to the world. It shows the world a love that is only possible through Christ and so commends the gospel.

Unity: Jesus prays for his disciples, which includes us, "I do not ask for these only, but also for those who will believe in me through their word, that they may all be one, just as you, Father, are in me, and I in you, that they also may be in us, so that the world may believe that you have sent me" (John 17:20–21). Our churches' unity presents a picture of the gospel to the watching world. Our unity shows the world that Jesus is truly from God, and it implicitly invites the world to trust in him.

Worship: Our churches' worship also has evangelistic power. Discussing the corporate proclamation of the Word by all the church's members, Paul says, "But if all prophesy, and an unbeliever or outsider enters, he is convicted by all, he is called to account by all, the secrets of his heart are disclosed, and so, falling on his face, he will worship God and declare that God is really among you" (1 Cor. 14:24–25). Our worship proclaims the reality of God, and it can and should have a powerful effect on unbelievers who experience it.

Sound doctrine empowers holiness, love, unity, and worship, and all of these magnify and adorn the church's witness to the gospel.

While these things certainly impact our lives as individuals, all of these fruits of sound doctrine are manifested most richly in the corporate life of the church. Love and unity are inherently corporate, and holiness and worship reach their fullest expression as we embody them together as a body. This means that our Christian witness consists of more than individual evangelism—it involves the entire life of the church. A church characterized by holiness, love, unity, and worship is a powerful testimony to the gospel. It adorns the gospel. It serves as a mirror for the gospel, holding up its transforming power for all to see. And sound doctrine shapes, renews, and empowers the corporate life and witness of the church.

EQUIP, MOTIVATE, AND CULTIVATE YOUR CHURCH'S WITNESS—THROUGH SOUND DOCTRINE

So pastors, equip your people to evangelize by giving them sound doctrine. Teach them the gospel over and over again so that they learn it by heart.[1] Consistently connect the dots between other biblical doctrines and the gospel, so that your people can explain the whole Christian worldview to their atheist friends and Muslim neighbors.

Further, motivate your people to evangelize through proclaiming gospel doctrine to them. We should be convicted over our lack of evangelism, but guilt will take us only so far, for so long. So boldly proclaim the love of Christ to your people until that love fills their hearts and overflows to their friends and neighbors.

In addition, carefully cultivate the corporate witness of your church. Your church's corporate life will either commend or contradict the gospel you preach. It will either promote Christ's reputation or smear it. Your church is much more than the sum of its parts: it's a mirror to reflect God's glory in the gospel, a broadcasting station to magnify and transmit the message of the cross.

Finally, use your church's corporate witness in evangelism. Teach your people that the church is Jesus's evangelism

---

[1] Two helpful tools for this are Greg Gilbert's book *What Is the Gospel?* (Wheaton, IL: Crossway, 2010) and the evangelistic resource *Two Ways to Live: Know and Share the Gospel* by Phillip D. Jensen and Tony Payne (Kingsford, AU: Matthias Media, 1989).

program. While keeping a clear line between the church and the world, invite non-Christians in to experience the corporate life of your church for themselves. Let them see your light and taste your saltiness (Matt. 5:13–16).

SOUND DOCTRINE: VOCABULARY FOR EVANGELISTIC IMPROVISATION

Unlike jazz improvisation, the message of the gospel is the same every time we preach it. Like a jazz performance, though, each evangelistic conversation will be different, and will force us to think on our feet and improvise.

Therefore, we should constantly be learning the "vocabulary" of the gospel. I don't mean just the theological terms bound up with the gospel, though those are important. Instead, I mean the message of the gospel itself, and all the biblical doctrines that support it, connect to it, frame it, and help make sense of it.

The better we know the gospel, the better we will share it. And the more our lives and churches conform to sound doctrine, the more we will commend the gospel we proclaim. Sound doctrine is for witness.

Postscript

SOUND DOCTRINE IS FOR JOY

Sound doctrine is the lifeblood of the church. It shapes and guides the church's teaching. It nourishes holiness. It fosters love. It grounds and repairs unity. It calls forth worship. And it informs and motivates our witness to the gospel.

Far from being an optional sideshow or a distraction from the church's real work, sound doctrine is essential for the life of the church. Sound doctrine gives us a road map for living lives and building up churches that please God. It lays before us the path of godly living. It provides the script for the Christian life, the music we dance to.

And the goal of such doctrine is that we, together with all the saints, would glorify God and find joy in him. Referring to all the teaching he gave his disciples on his last night with them, Jesus says, "These things I have spoken to you, that my joy may be in you, and that your joy may be full" (John 15:11). Jesus taught his disciples rich doctrinal truths so that his own joy would live in the disciples, and the disciples' joy would be filled up.

Because it unfolds the riches of God's grace to us, sound doctrine brings light and hope and joy. It fills our hearts with satisfaction in Christ because of what he has done for us. Sound doctrine is for joy.

At the beginning of 1 John, the apostle John testifies that he is an eyewitness of the Son, and then, echoing Jesus, he says, "And we are writing these things so that our joy may be complete" (1 John 1:4). John's joy in the truth needed to spill over to other believers. If it didn't, his joy would have been incomplete.

So it is with us. Sound doctrine should shape our lives, and our lives should be shaped by the church, and help shape the church. The joy we have in God through sound doctrine is made complete when we share our joy with our brothers and sisters in the fellowship of the church.

Do you want joy in God? Then devote yourself to studying sound doctrine and living the life it marks out for you. And do all of this together with the other members of your church. You will find that, as your joy in God overflows to others, it will grow steadily fuller.

Sound doctrine is for life—life in the church, the life of the church, and beyond.

SPECIAL THANKS

Thanks first of all to Mark Dever, Matt Schmucker, Ryan Townsend, and Jonathan Leeman for your godly leadership not only in your own local church, but also in and through 9Marks. Thank you for giving me the privilege and joy of laboring with you all. I am grateful to God for the ways that you have helped me grow as a Christian, and for the ways you have given selflessly to me and my family. And a special thanks to Jonathan for investing so much in order to help me grow as a writer.

Thank you to all the 9Marks staff for making this work of building healthy churches happen. And thank you to all the donors who give your resources to this work so that we can give our time.

Thank you, Crossway, for your helpful and valuable partnership with our ministry.

Thank you to Ligon Duncan, whose address at T4G '08 planted some of the seeds that eventually grew into this book.

Thanks to those who read and provided feedback on the manuscript, including my parents and my dear friends Mike Carnicella, Matt McCullough, and Alex Duke.

Thank you to my fellow members of Third Avenue Baptist

Church for your commitment to the gospel and to each other, and for living godly lives that are rooted in the soil of sound doctrine.

Thanks, finally, to my wife Kristin, who simply cannot be thanked enough.

GENERAL INDEX

accountability, 26

baptism, 75, 78, 88
bitterness, 71, 78, 81

Carson, D. A., 85
church
  as the body of Christ, 76–77
  growth of, 23–24
  membership in, 24, 108
  traditions of, 41
  unity in, 73–82, 102–3
creation, 32, 99

discipleship, 22, 24, 44–45
Duncan, Ligon, 88

Edwards, Jonathan, 69–70
envy, 78
eschatology, 56–57
evangelism, 95–105

faith, 19–20, 51, 75, 81
fall, 32
false doctrine, 20, 41–42,
  66–67
forgiveness, 35, 49, 96–97

Gilbert, Greg, 104n

God
  character of, 36–37, 51,
    89–90
  covenant promises of, 34,
    97–98
  glory of, 13, 55, 91
  image of, 40, 67, 71–72
  justice of, 32, 38, 55–56
  knowledge of, 18, 30, 37–38,
    54
  obedience to, 86–87
gospel transformation, 24–25,
  29, 82, 96–100
gossip, 78
grace, 51, 75, 85, 94, 101, 108
Grudem, Wayne, 38n, 48

holiness, 35, 47–61, 102, 107
Holy Spirit, 31–32, 68, 78–79
Horton, Michael, 30n, 33
humility, 79–80

idolatry, 88, 98
Irenaeus of Lyons, 10

Jensen, Phillip D., 104n
Jesus
  image of, 39, 55, 61
  incarnation of, 80

SCRIPTURE INDEX

9MARKS: BUILDING HEALTHY CHURCHES SERIES

Based on Mark Dever's best-selling book *Nine Marks of a Healthy Church*, each book in this series helps readers grasp basic biblical commands regarding the local church.

TITLES INCLUDE:

Biblical Theology	Conversion	The Gospel
Church Discipline	Discipling	Missions
Church Elders	Evangelism	Prayer
Church Membership	Expositional Preaching	Sound Doctrine

For more information, visit crossway.org.
For translated versions of these and other 9Marks books, visit 9Marks.org/bookstore/translations.

9Marks

Building Healthy Churches

9Marks exists to equip church leaders with a biblical vision and practical resources for displaying God's glory to the nations through healthy churches.

To that end, we want to see churches characterized by these nine marks of health:

1 Expositional Preaching
2 Biblical Theology
3 A Biblical Understanding of the Gospel
4 A Biblical Understanding of Conversion
5 A Biblical Understanding of Evangelism
6 Biblical Church Membership
7 Biblical Church Discipline
8 Biblical Discipleship
9 Biblical Church Leadership

Find all our Crossway titles
and other resources at
www.9Marks.org